OUTDOOR
CLASSROOMS

a handbook for school gardens

Based on a gate in
The Ian Potter Foundation Children's Garden
at the Royal Botanic Gardens Melbourne

Carolyn Nuttall and Janet Millington

Illustrations by

Mary-Anne Cotter, Kay Schiefelbein and Jane Bottomley

Published by
Permanent Publications
Hyden House Ltd
The Sustainability Centre
East Meon, Hampshire GU32 1HR, UK
Tel: 01730 823 311
Fax: 01730 823 322
Overseas: (international code +44 - 1730)
info@permaculture.co.uk
www.permanentpublications.co.uk

Distributed in the USA by
Chelsea Green Publishing Company, PO Box 428, White River Junction, VT 05001
www.chelseagreen.com

Published in association with
Permaculture Association, London WC1N 3XX
office@permaculture.org.uk www.permaculture.org.uk

First published in Australia 2008, 2nd edition 2012
First published in the UK 2013, reprinted 2016

Design and layout:	John Dick, www.piproductions.com.au
Cover Illustration:	Mary-Anne Cotter
Editor:	Robyn Cook
Illustrations:	Mary-Anne Cotter, Janet Millington, Kay Schiefelbein, Jane Bottomley
Photographers:	John Dick, Janet Millington, Bruce Molloy
Support:	Sustainability @ James Cook University, www.jcu.edu.au/tropeco

Printed in the UK by CPI Antony Rowe, Chippenham, Wiltshire

All paper from FSC certified mixed sources

The Forest Stewardship Council (FSC) is a non-profit international organisation established to promote the
responsible management of the world's forests. Products carrying the FSC label are independently certified to
assure consumers that they come from forests that are managed to meet the social, economic and ecological
needs of present and future generations.

British Library Cataloguing-in-Publication Data
A catalogue record for this book is available from the British Library

ISBN 978 1 85623 113 8

Disclaimer
All due care and attention has been taken in the production of this book. The opinions expressed in it are those of the authors.
All details given in this book were correct at the time of publication. All care has been taken in the preparation of the information herein,
but no responsibility can be accepted by the publisher or authors for any damages resulting from the misinterpretation of this work.

Dedications

This book is dedicated to my mother Elizabeth Alice Nuttall, nee Covington, for her loving support.

This book is also dedicated to Stephen Denovan, the boy who found his way because of the school garden.

Carolyn Nuttall

I dedicate this work to all learners who teach and teachers who learn.

With thanks to those who taught me some of life's most wonderous lessons, my mum and dad and husband Mick. Special thanks to my children Katie and David, who gave, and continue to give me such joy and wonderful memories of our times together... outdoors.

Janet Millington

Acknowledgements

I wish to thank my teacher friends, Rosie O'Brien who had words to fill the spaces and Pat Hong who replied with a wise head when the writing needed a listener. As well, I thank my niece Cecelia Nuttall for her help and a special gratitude to my co-writer, Janet Millington for her friendship, good cheer and hard work on this book.

Carolyn Nuttall

To Bill Mollison and David Holmgren who saw in the 1970s how we would need to build sustainable communities and make children responsible and self reliant.

I wish to acknowledge Fiona Ball and her early permaculture school gardens and Permikids and Leonie Shanahan for her passionate effort to have kids eating real food grown in flourishing permaculture gardens.

I acknowledge the support of North Arm and Eumundi State Schools who deliver inspirational educational programs and who have embraced so well the concept of outdoor classrooms.

I must also acknowledge the wonderful mind and good intent of my co-writer Carolyn for whom I have the greatest respect and to thank her for her confidence in me and our friendship that has grown during the writing.

Janet Millington

Contents

Preface

About this book

- 🐦 Although written for formally qualified teachers, we strive to engage with all who work with children.

- 🐦 We offer information for the development and use of the outdoors for teaching purposes. It is a range of opportunities rather than prescribed requirements.

- 🐦 Our intention is to extend thinking and practice based on a new plan with new resources.

- 🐦 It does not contain a large body of information about plants. This is considered to be easily accessible from other sources.

- 🐦 The ideas are often fanciful but we believe are attainable at some level.

- 🐦 We acknowledge that each school community is unique and that one size will not fit all.

- 🐦 It is our hope that teachers, who are the architects and designers of the learning environment, will look to the outdoors for inspiration.

Introduction

How many teachers does it take to explain a school garden?

Well, in this case, two!

We are primary school teachers with over 60 years of teaching experience between us, many of which have been in garden-based learning. We have made the gardens and seen the benefits for the students. We have celebrated with the teachers who have found new energy and inspiration for the teaching task and we have watched as the community looked with pride over the children's progress. These events have revealed to us the value and potential of gardens in schools. Our motivation now in our retirement years is to continue our connection with schools and to write this book because the lessons to be learned from a school garden have never been more critical than they are today.

Educators cannot stand aloof from the important decisions that need to be made. We face a future of declining oil supplies and a climate change that is set to affect our lives in significant ways. Schools will be called upon to embrace the national goal of environmental education for sustainability, a preparation and empowerment of students to assume responsibility for creating and enjoying a sustainable future. Teachers will be expected to design teaching and learning strategies to achieve these outcomes. The challenge is enormous because it is transformative on many levels.

It is our hope that this book will help to guide the way in these transitional times. We know that a school permaculture garden, as simple as the ideas seems, has the features for success in this challenge.

The book is a compilation of writings from two people with different experiences and expertise. The reader will be aware of some overlap and our different approaches but they will clearly see our shared passion for school gardens. We see the diversity as a positive feature of the book.

It suggests that there are multiple pathways in the process of gardening at school and that the reader will confidently find ideas from many people to create the garden and teaching plan to suit their own situation.

In Janet's work you will find a full and detailed plan for developing a permaculture garden; its establishment, design, maintenance and curriculum links. The advice is practical and useful and teachers will find the curriculum resources that she has included to be directly applicable and time saving. Janet is a teacher with a deep understanding of the natural world developed through years of application of permaculture principles to landuse, including those in the schoolyard. She has designed whole school environments, school gardens, curricula, units of study and lesson plans. More recently, Janet has trained teachers in the vocational education sector and has helped to write the national Accedited Permaculture Training. She is an inspired educator for whom artist Kay Schiefelbein creates engaging images that support the ideas and concepts in her text.

Carolyn has a slightly different focus, though she too has a permaculture background. She starts with a look at the history of school gardens and the reasons for their revival. Her garden world is about empowering teachers and children to move learning into the outdoors as it is here that children can easily take hold of their own learning and to share with their teachers the associated tasks, ideas, planning and implementation. She delves into the fanciful and imagines outdoor classrooms that make the schoolyard a more inspiring place for the young; a place where they can play, work and imagine and regain what they are losing every day – their connection to a natural environment. The artist Mary-Anne Cotter has created inspiring images from these imaginings.

You and the children you teach are warmly welcome to step into the Outdoor Classroom.

Carolyn and Janet

Imagining a School of the Future with Multiple Outdoor Classrooms

This illustration gives some idea of what a school that is landscaped for learning might look like. This school is a collection of energy efficient, high tech, solar passive buildings in a farm-like setting. Classrooms have courtyards for easy access to the outdoors and the schoolyard beyond the classrooms is an adventurous landscape for work and play. Here children interact with a natural environment on a daily basis and learn the lessons of life and living through play, hands-on experiences and specific studies.

The school ground is valued as a setting for curriculum development and teachers in this school see this space as an extension to their classroom. They develop multiple outdoor classrooms that are learning areas for specific curriculum subjects or just natural places for imaginative play. In this schoolyard, there is room to raise animals, make gardens, compost, recycle, fly a kite, play a game or just listen to a story under a big tree.

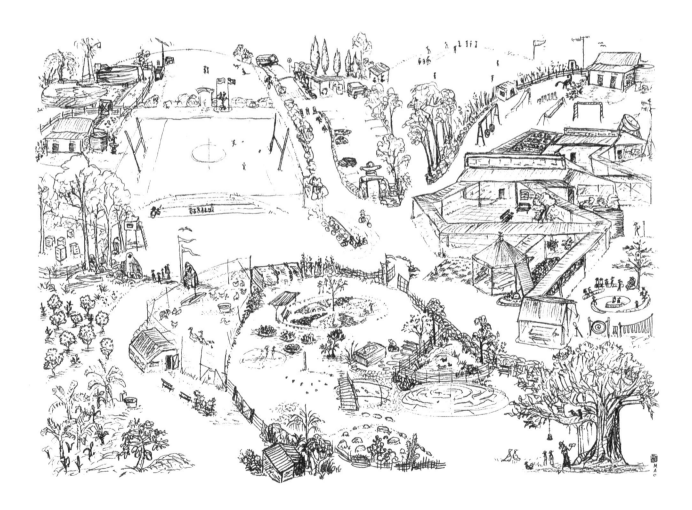

Part I

New visions for old school grounds

Potted history of school gardens

Revival of school gardens

Value of school gardens

Teaching and learning in the outdoors

New Visions for Old School Grounds

The time has come to build new visions for school grounds. If we value authentic experiences for children, we would not lock up the schoolyard and drive the children inside. We would design their school environment to connect them to the richness of their world, to nature and the landscapes that we know reflect their interests and make meaning for them.

The school ground is a prime resource for all schools and traditionally its development has been for sport and gymnastic play. Schools on the whole make good provision for these needs of the child but the school ground has always been more than ovals and climbing frames.

Teachers have always known the value of a walk in the outdoors to collect or observe something in nature and have made good use of the schoolyard for their own purposes. And children have always used the playground for their lunchtime adventures among the natural features of the landscape. It is their outdoor classroom because learning also happens in the schoolyard. Children are learning all the time.

We take the wisdom of age-old practices to create visions of grounds that fulfil the needs of teachers, to find in the school landscape, a natural diversity to enhance the development of the child's environmental awareness through actual contact with the elements of that landscape.

These same landscapes can serve the needs of the child to play in natural areas among the plants and in the soil, to play creatively and safely, developing through their own resources, their own environmental awareness.

The schoolyard is an important place for the young and it can hold more than we traditionally assign to it. Children love to play sport and climb on the playground equipment but the modern child may need more. It may fall upon schools to add an environmental quality to the playground in light of the deficient opportunities that the urban child has for such connection. For the health of the modern child and, it could be argued, the modern ecology, it may become the duty of educators to provide, on campus, the means for children to have quality outdoor experiences on a daily basis and the wisdom to use them as teaching and learning opportunities.

The issues of environmental awareness and quality are not unconsidered in the modern school. The naturalisation of the school ground and its use as a teaching site has begun through projects such as school gardens, learnscaping and revegetation programs. These have been important pioneer activities in building a vision that school grounds can be developed for educational purposes, that grounds are a rich resource to support learning in curriculum subjects and that curriculum development and grounds development can be in partnership.

The call is for a new vision for school grounds – a new perception of how the grounds will look, what they will contain and how they will fit into the learning agenda.

Before going forward, it would be appropriate at this point to look at the history of the school garden and the forces that influenced its rise and fall over time. The following account is a brief explanation and I apologise to any whose contribution I have overlooked.

A Potted History of School Gardens

Norwood Infant School garden, 1912-1913

It is said that there is nothing new in education and this is true of the arrival of the school garden. The vegetable plot has been a feature of schools in Australia for all time, albeit moving in and out of favour over the years.

As early as 1902, gardens were a common feature of schools in Victoria. In that era, a 'new' system of education was implemented in Victorian State Schools following a Royal Commission inquiry into Technical Education. The 'new' system was based on progressive trends developed in Europe and England and preached, as its first principle, the importance of learning through experience. One of the Commission's recommendations was the cultivation of school gardens.

In Queensland, there has been a long history of agricultural activities at school. The Project Club Branch, within the Department of Education, supported many clubs in schools throughout the state for several decades after World War 11. During this time the vegetable plot was very popular but it was soon to lie fallow as syllabus changes were introduced.

By the late 1960s, man had walked on the moon and the race for the minds of children lay in the future of science and mathematics teaching. The school garden, a relic of a past era, was rarely seen in the schoolground.

New syllabuses, new methodology and new-style open classrooms appeared in the 1970s. Old schools opened up their dividing doors and new schools were built. The era of open classrooms arrived and the classroom was the focus for all learning. The school garden took a back seat, in Queensland at least, to Cuisenaire rods and Dick and Dora.

As in agriculture, a fallow time for the school garden was of great benefit, as school gardens were to re-emerge several decades later, enriched with a new vigour and a new pedagogy.

In this interim, beginning in the 1970s, there was a re-articulation of issues relating to school environments and what constituted a good climate for optimal child development. Topics discussed in universities and colleges at that time included individual differences, learning styles, experiential learning and children's sense of place. The focus was on child-centred learning and the debate was long and lasting.

In this same decade, Permaculture was launched. This is a design system conceived by Bill Mollison and David Holmgren for creating sustainable human environments. It includes as one of its principles, the bringing of food growing back to the cities. Permaculture designers and educators have been important pioneers in the setting up of food gardens in schools.

Beginning in the 1980s, graduates of Permaculture Design Courses (usually parents of the children in the school) have sought permission from principals to set up gardens and composting systems in the schoolyard. The knowledge of garden design and the preservation and extension of natural systems brought into schools by these people has been significant, so much so, that permaculture is well established as the preferred design for school gardens today.

In 1981, enthusiastic community members established one of the first of the modern era school gardens at Black Forest Primary School in Adelaide. Now run by an enthusiastic teacher and involving all year levels, this fine example of a school garden has welcomed many visitors through its gates.

In 1986, Learning Through Landscapes, a research project set up by county councils and the Department of Education and Science in the United Kingdom, was established. This initiative addressed two issues: how to extend educational opportunities and how to improve environmental quality in school grounds. This organisation remains active today.

In this same decade in Australia, environmental education syllabuses were introduced and outdoor environmental education centres were established. These delivered a highly effective education program for schools and communities. They put in place a strong ecological focus for schools.

Learnscapes: A New Idea for Learning

In 1991, Malcolm Cox introduced the word 'learnscapes'* to label his general thesis that schools can develop their grounds to make better educational use of them.

The word 'learnscape', an amalgamation of 'learn' and 'landscape', illuminates by association, a connection between learning and landscaping. Cox proposed that grounds development become a partner with curriculum development and that the academic learning of the classroom be supported by specifically designed sites in the school ground.

Learnscaping theory extends beyond school gardens but it is the important platform upon which the concept of school gardens is built.

* IMAGINE… School Grounds as 'Learnscapes', Mt Coot-tha Botanic Gardens. 1991

The learnscaping concept was adopted by the New South Wales Department of Education and Training (DET) as an environmental education initiative. This followed an initiative called Greening Schools, which was set up early in the decade and ran for a few years. Learnscaping became a strong focus and under the direction of Syd Smith, a chief educational officer, the planning and design of this strategy was widely applied.

An early and award winning design for a learnscaped school was at Harwood Island Public School in northern NSW. Helen Tyas Tunggal, the principal at that time, has further developed the theory and application of learnscaping, first through The Learnscapes Trust and now Learnscapes Planning and Design based in Angourie in NSW.

In 1998 DET funded 15 schools to set up learnscaping projects and these became part of a study by researchers, Skamp and Bergmann, from the School of Education, Southern Cross University. The study looked at teachers' perceptions of the value and impacts of learnscaping.

In 1992, I entered the field of outdoor learning when my class of young children created an edible garden in the school ground. I documented this story in a book published in 1996, A Children's Food Forest: An Outdoor Classroom. I followed this in 1999 with the publication of support materials for the school garden called The Environmental Workshop, which was reprinted in 2003 as The Food Forest Resource Sheets.

For five years from 1995 to 2000 when it ceased publication, Mary-Anne Cotter, an illustrator of this book and I wrote a kid's page called Food Foresters for the Permaculture International Journal. It targeted young people who were interested in gardening at school and at home.

Developing School Gardens with Permaculture

By the mid 1990s, many school gardens had been created. Permaculture people were leading the way. They explored the scope of the garden to raise children's awareness of growing their own food using organic and earth friendly techniques.

In 1995, Robina McCurdy, a New Zealand educator, offered a workshop on school gardens at Black Forest Primary, immediately prior to the Australian Permaculture Conference in Adelaide. Robina has been a strong leader in this field and her work has been wide-ranging and important in the development of the school garden concept.

Sally Ramsden, another pioneer in the promotion of school gardens created Zone C, a special zone for children in permaculture planning.

Support for outdoor environmental education increased in the 1990s. Environmental education centres expanded their programs and government departments, local councils and community groups addressed environmental issues through the development of resources for schools.

These covered land-care issues, water and energy watch programs, waste management and recycling, environmental awareness, preservation of native habitat, repair of natural areas and the learnscaping of school grounds. Groups concerned with rural revitalisation were giving encouragement to schools to 'farm' their schoolyards.

In 1995, the US educator Steve van Matre toured Australia to promote his book 'Earth Education; A New Beginning' 1990. He argued that environmental education had gone astray, that it was in fact 'environmental miseducation' as it failed to address the environmental issues with enough urgency. He said that environmental education in the USA was being 'co-opted, diluted and trivialised'. Van Matre offers an alternative approach that immerses children in outdoor adventures that are infused with the ideals of deep ecology. His ideas have influenced many educators.

In 1997, members of Permaculture Noosa (Queensland), Janet Millington, the co-author of this book and Fiona Ball created Permi Kids. Fiona and Leonie Shanahan ran and continue to run special fun programs in gardening and the visual and performing arts for children in schools, weekend workshops and events at fairs and festivals.

Other educators who have made a lasting contribution to children's learning about food issues are Jacqui Hunter of Hunter Gatherer Designs (huntergd@chariot.net.au) based in Adelaide, South Australia, and Jude Fanton of Seed Savers Network, Byron Bay, New South Wales (www.seedsavers.net). Both have produced resources for garden-based learning in schools.

New Millennium, New Interest

The new millennium arrived and interest in school gardens was growing. It looked as if it would be a steady but slow process to raise awareness in schools of the value of outdoor learning, but events were set to change. A new player entered the scene with new imperatives and new methods for teaching. A restaurateur was set to have her say.

In Melbourne in 2001, Stephanie Alexander, a chef and food book author, left her kitchen bench for a walk through the school gate. Few people have been so bold. She wanted to *"get the children gardening and cooking in order to teach them about the joys and benefits of freshly grown food"* (Kitchen Garden Cooking with Kids, 2006,viii).

A successful kitchen garden was established at Collingwood College in inner city Melbourne and in 2004 the Stephanie Alexander Kitchen Garden Foundation was set up to promote the kitchen/ garden concept and to expand it into other schools.

Through the efforts of Stephanie and her foundation, the profile of the school garden, as a significant part of a well-balanced curriculum for schools, has been significantly raised. She offers a model that adds to the range of approaches that are available for school garden education. Governments at the highest level are listening and allocating substantial funds for other states to follow this example.

Around the same time in Melbourne, an organisation that supports the development of community food gardens on government housing estates – Cultivating Community – developed their own approach to educational gardening and are currently active in a number of Melbourne schools. They initially worked with Stephanie Alexander in the school garden at Collingwood College.

Educating for Sustainability

In 2003, the Australian Government published, Educating for a Sustainable Future, a National Environmental Education Statement for Australian Schools. It provides a nationally agreed upon vision for environmental education for all states.

Governments were looking for broad changes in education, new action in teaching and learning and the raising of ecological awareness. This constitutes a new literacy, an eco-literacy, and

teachers will be called upon to effect these changes.

The move towards sustainability foreshadows a major shift in education. The school garden, as simple as the idea seems, is, I believe, well positioned to backdrop the values change and the move to environmental education for sustainability that schools are being encouraged to implement.

Support for teachers is coming from a variety of sources and in a variety of forms. Teachers are being offered professional training, networking opportunities, conferences, resource materials and assistance from local groups and private consultants.

Much of the long-term work has been offered by community organisations such as the Australian City Farms and Community Gardens Network (www.communitygarden.org.au), Cultivating Communities in Melbourne (www.cultivatingcommunity .org.au),
Growing Communities in Brisbane (www.northey streetcityfarm.org.au),
CareDesign in the Illawarra, NSW, Learning in the Garden in South Australia and regional permaculture groups all over Australia (www.permaculture international.org).
They are all delivering support for garden programs in schools. This list is not exhaustive. Many more groups are working with schools today.

The school garden has a growing list of supporters; state, federal and local governments, political parties, educators, business and agricultural organisations, parent groups, environmentalists, permaculturalists, nutritionists, the good food/ good health lobby, tuckshop groups, community farming groups, the slow food movement, learnscapers and sustainable schools groups.

Obesity and Poor Nutrition

Obesity and poor nutrition are issues affecting children in Australia today. Many schools are building school gardens to showcase fresh food ideas in their healthy eating programs. Tuckshops are changing their menus for better food choices and to raise awareness of food issues. These are important programs and with the current focus on funding opportunities in the area of fresh food education, kitchen gardens and good health concepts, school gardens will be appearing in many more schools.

Uncertain Times

We are living in a time of great uncertainty. The ecological health of the planet is well documented: global warming, declining resources, degradation of the land and waterways, population growth, fresh water shortage, loss of bio-diversity, peak oil, food and health issues. The damage is done and the design for the collective behaviour that is required to fix our environment is gradually being put into place.

The community expects behavioural change to begin in school, and we do see a lot of energy around the issues of waste reduction, water and energy conservation and transport solutions.

All of these issues have found their way into schools in recent times. But the school garden promises the child a lot more than what the community hopes for.

Teachers know that children learn well when they are engaged in projects like gardening and it will be from this base that we may see changes in the way teachers work and the way children learn.

It may be that the humble vegetable garden in the schoolyard of every child is where children build their environmental awareness and skills base to live comfortably with uncertainty, to live without fear and ineptitude but with optimism and competency and an understanding of what constitutes their wellbeing.

Futurists draw our attention to the rise and dominance of the biological sciences in research programs. The school garden, the place where the early lessons in biology begin, may be well positioned for the future needs of the modern student. It may also be the time for schools to begin serious programs in moral education, teaching ethics, principles, values and virtues to enable the current generation of students to be part of the debate as the biological scientists take their knowledge beyond the realms of what we know.

The Revival of School Gardens

From Darwin to the Derwent, children are farming their school grounds and teachers are harvesting their work for teaching and learning opportunities.

It is no surprise that gardens are springing up in schools all over the country. The revival of school gardens has been driven by the efforts of a diverse group of stakeholders both within and outside of the school system. The input from these groups has meant that school gardens have re-emerged with a new vigour, pedagogy, gardening technique and urgency.

It is not a local phenomenon. Children all over the world, in countries rich and poor, are gardening at school. It is a global trend driven by global urgencies, at times hunger but more often environmental and health issues. Add climate change and energy descent (due to the likely impact of the peaking in production of the global oil supply) to this list and it may be that school gardens will receive even greater attention in the coming years.

The trend to revive the school garden is set to continue as there is a growing acceptance that a garden is a proper feature of a school ground and an integral part of a well-balanced curriculum. Education initiatives such as New Basics, Essential Learnings and Sustainable Schools will utilise the school garden as a scaffold upon which their initiatives can be developed in some way.

Children love gardens and their enthusiasm bodes well for the revival. The garden is a place in the schoolyard that they can call their own. The childish plot* looks set to be a common feature of school grounds for some time.

*Acknowledging Spensley Primary School garden in Clifton Hill, Melbourne.

The Value of School Gardens

"Gardens are valued as places for reflection and for peace, places where we can be refreshed and nourished by nature."

Helen Cushing (Beyond Organics, 2005; 28)

Research Validates School Gardening

There is growing evidence of the value of school gardens. Most of it is still anecdotal but similar outcomes are being recorded throughout Australia and overseas. The evidence from those who work with children in school gardens and the children themselves is overwhelmingly positive and strong. The responses gathered by teachers working in the area is valuable indeed, and teachers wishing to start a garden should feel confident to proceed on the basis of this empirical research. Scientific evidence of the value of school gardens is in the early stages of investigation and its findings will inform teacher's practice in the years ahead.

The anecdoted benefits of learning in the garden are wide reaching and extend to students' academic results, their social and personal development and their understanding of food and environmental issues. Some observers talk of school health and better community connections. Teachers speak of a renewed energy for the teaching task and a welcome increase in ideas for structuring the learning process.

The positive potential of the school garden is yet to be fully understood. We proceed knowing that gardens exert important positive effects on people because they are a setting for creativity, pleasure and harmony. And gardens reach beyond their edges to the whole of nature and are thus connected to the greater universe, including the spiritual.

Not to put too high a shine on it, not all school gardens achieve this level of bliss. As in any human endeavour, there are issues that will work against success. In a school situation, these have been identified as children's unreadiness for the task, time constraints, motivation of teachers, support from principals and succession issues. The bigger issues of water restrictions, lack of knowledge about gardening, crop failure and financial constraints appear not to be impediments to successful gardening at school.

The following is a collection of short glimpses of the attributes of a school garden and the benefits they bring. This is followed by ideas listed with bullet points for ease of reading. The value and benefits of school gardens is far reaching and it would need more space than I have, to cover it comprehensively.

For the Child

The Garden Joy

There is joyous wonder in watching a plant grow from seed. We must respect this wonder and encourage the child's curiosity and interest in the natural world. It is in their nature to learn and a garden is a learning place for every child.

Hands-on Learning

School gardens are a setting for learning in the environment, as opposed to learning about the environment. Here, children, in a first hand way, learn about the diversity of plants and animals, their lifecycles and the growth and decay of all living things.

Here, they get close to the natural elements – the soil, water, and sunshine of the garden. And here they learn to watch the weather and plan for seasonal change.

In a garden, children begin to form a deep understanding of the ecology of which they are part by observing at close quarters the behaviours of living things, including themselves.

Skills for Living

Gardening is a life skill. Learning strategies associated with planning, building and caring for a garden are skills that children will carry into adulthood. The garden is a living system and work in the garden is a creative role for children and adults alike.

In its broadest sense, the garden is a connection to the forces that govern our lives – the natural elements, the social and environmental systems and the living Earth. Gardening is an endeavour that involves the mind, body and the spirit, with gardens nurturing both child and teacher.

Garden-work for Children

Children can increase their physical activity, fitness, dexterity, skill and contribution through work in the garden. They can learn to use tools and become skilled in doing useful work.

Children can rediscover what many have lost, that sense of contribution to family life by doing household jobs.

Food Issues

The school garden is part of a healthy eating program. Children have been known to try something new if they have grown it.

By growing some of their own food, children form an understanding of food issues: where food comes from, what the plants look like, what part of a plant is edible and the names of plants.

They are also exposed to the diversity of food crops and the idea that people from other cultures may eat different plants. Importantly, they learn that they can grow food and that they can acquire the skills to be producers as well as consumers. They can learn how to prepare the food grown at school and they can dine on it and share it with others.

The Quest for the Self-Disciplined Child

Work in the garden develops in children skills of self-management. Not all children reach this level of development.

Said the teacher to the disruptive child: *"Who's in charge of you?"* The child replies, *"You!" "No,"* said the teacher, *"not me."* The child tries again, *"Mum." "No,"* said the teacher, *"you are. You are in charge of yourself and you should be telling yourself to behave well."*

For the Teacher

Gardens and Teaching

Teachers can use the garden setting to extend the range of learning styles employed in the teaching process. These can include hands-on, inquiry-based, problem-based and child-initiated learning; techniques easily applied in an outdoor classroom.

Gardens and Curriculum

School garden programs vary widely in scope. In some schools, the activities of the garden are connected to a wide range of curriculum subjects whereas others use it only as a resource in the teaching of science, maths and nutrition for example. In some cases, a food garden stands alone as an activity with its own status and its own set of essential learnings.

Work in a garden is a cross-curricula activity. Learning in the garden winds its way through the curriculum, picking up the subject requirements as it attends to the needs of the garden. It is a trail that intertwines the disciplines, dissolving subject boundaries in its wake, leaving the teacher the task of untangling it to find the curriculum connections.

This process appeals to the many teachers who enjoy the richness of the teaching task when unrestricted by subject frameworks.

A Garden Extends Beyond Its Edges

We can teach children that their gardens extend far beyond their edges, that the good they do in the garden will be good for the whole environment. They can know that when they use earth-friendly systems to make the plants grow and to attract wildlife, their garden becomes part of the natural world – a little patch in the schoolyard for the wildlife of the local area to find food and shelter.

Ownership

School gardens bring benefits when the teacher sets up the learning environment to enable children to fully participate in the process. Full participation includes ownership, management, decision-making, physical work, care of and responsibility for the garden. When it is a children's garden, the benefits are abundant.

The full range of the values and benefits of a school garden is broad and for ease of reading, they are organised into lists. These are not exhaustive. Who knows the full effects of a garden on a child's psyche!

SURVEYOR

Pedagogical Benefits

The teacher can offer a broad range of learning styles in a garden setting.

- ❀ active
- ❀ hands-on
- ❀ experiential
- ❀ real life
- ❀ child-centred
- ❀ child-initiated
- ❀ collaborative
- ❀ Integrated
- ❀ problem based
- ❀ Inquiry based
- ❀ place based
- ❀ trial and error

The garden activity helps the teacher to look at curriculum in broad ways.

- ❀ multiple curriculum links
- ❀ cross-curricular activities
- ❀ Incidental learning
- ❀ Integrated/ holistic approach
- ❀ abundant new ideas for planning
- ❀ programs for all learners

School gardens help children to get more one-to-one time with teachers.

- ❀ better performance in core subjects
- ❀ development of thinking skills
- ❀ boosts thirst for knowledge
- ❀ better performance on standard tests
- ❀ deeper understandings
- ❀ deeper questions
- ❀ self-assessing skills
- ❀ success for all children
- ❀ opportunities for practical learners

RESEARCHER

Teachers share the teaching and learning tasks with children who run a garden project.

- ❀ stewardship responsibilities
- ❀ Increased responsibilities and rights
- ❀ sense of contribution
- ❀ sense of belonging
- ❀ awareness of interconnections
- ❀ respect for others and their rights
- ❀ Increase in awareness of food issues
- ❀ ownership of their own learning
- ❀ pupil/ teacher power relationship
- ❀ opportunity to initiate own learning
- ❀ learning life skills
- ❀ care-of-earth ethic

SEED SAVER

Children learn from many people when they create a garden.

- teachers
- permaculturalists
- cooks
- gardeners
- parents
- peer group
- specialists
- community people
- elders
- cultural groups
- Indigenous groups

CHEF

The school garden is valued by the children.

- for work and play
- ownership
- extended use of the playground
- naturalisation of schoolyard
- Improved environmental quality
- better play opportunities
- more plants and animals
- micro-climates with shade/ water
- creation of ambiance and mood
- site for outdoor classrooms
- sanctuary for wildlife
- flowers for the classroom
- welcoming of the visitor

School gardens are important in the physical development of the child.

- fresh air
- working with mind and body
- Increase in personal health through healthy eating
- exercise
- new skills (building/ tool handling)

Children learn important social roles when they grow, harvest and prepare food.

- citizenship
- dining skills
- co-operation and collaboration
- encouragement of memory and continuity
- Inclusiveness
- gardens reach beyond their edges
- growing food locally
- networking internationally
- energy and water watch
- recycling/ reusing
- sharing surplus
- to the community
- to whole of nature

School gardens can improve the health of a school.

- Improved attendance
- reduced boredom
- reduced bullying
- Improved behaviour
- less vandalism
- fewer playground incidents
- pride and performance

Children gain deeper understandings of issues.

- where food comes from
- weather, seasons and life cycles
- words and expression
- the ecology of the schoolyard
- the self, of capability and own direction
- how to work collaboratively
- permaculture solutions
- local and global issues

A garden is a setting for teaching.

- moral development
- solution-based learning
- applied higher level thinking skills
- responsible action
- Inclusiveness
- ethical understanding
- virtues
- values
- principles
- authority
- freedom
- peace

Selection of key benefits of school gardens.

- growing fresh and healthy food to eat
- learning about food
- hands-on learning
- child-driven learning ideas
- physical work
- moral development
- caters for the child who learns best in the practical world
- sense of pride
- place to welcome visitors
- opportunities for spontaneous and Incidental learning
- deeper ecological understanding
- a place in the grounds for children to manage
- a place to learn

Teaching and Learning in the Outdoors

"Children have a native tendency to learn by doing, to explore, to manipulate tools, to construct and give expression to joyous emotion."

John Dewey, 1916

Teachers have not lost sight of this wisdom, though the achievement of these ideals can be difficult to realise in the traditional classroom. The answer may lie in re-visioning the concept of 'where children learn', because it would seem that where they learn does influence how they learn. Teachers are discovering that they can embed experiential learning into their curriculum programs when they use gardens and other outdoor learning adventures as the contexts for learning.

There are multiple pathways to learning, some easier to organise than others. All teachers know that children learn by doing and discovered knowledge is the joy of every child. They also know how difficult it can be to set up materials for all children to work in this mode. There are always limitations of space in the classroom, and/ or a shortage of materials and supervision. In the outdoors, these restrictions do not always apply.

The following is the story of the children's garden at Seville Road State School. I use it to explain something of the process of how the outdoors can be a setting for discovered learning.

The Seville Road Story

In 1992, I encouraged the students in my Year 5/6 class in a Brisbane suburban school to make a vegetable garden in an out-of-the-way area of the school ground. It was a suggestion made in response to their request to make a rainforest. At the time I thought it would be a simple exercise, nothing more than a small garden for them to grow a few plants, but this was not to be. We had unknowingly embarked on a process that would alter the very nature of how I taught and how the children learned. We were experimenting with child-initiated experiential learning and it was revealing on many levels. This is their story.

The Children Take the Lead

After the successful establishment of a small plot of tomatoes and strawberries, I agreed with their plan to expand the garden and plant a few fruit trees. Assistance was sought to dig the holes in the heavily compacted soil. The children planted, mulched and named their trees and pledged to care for them.

I agreed that a scarecrow would look good in the garden and, yes, a pond would be great as well. Introducing chickens into the garden was a big decision and one that extended my skills to the limit, but we got it going. Then there was the irrigation system designed by one of the boys who organised his gang to install it. (I got maths lessons out of this activity.) The girls had an idea to paint a mural on a block wall at the edge of the garden to designate its function and display its name. It was called The Food Forest and it was dedicated to growing edible plants.

Other kids came to see and play in the food forest and the kids in my class made rules for the visitors. They had to be reminded at times to welcome everyone and this they did, but there was always a well-established understanding of ownership and this bode well for the success of the garden.

The children ran a weekly club meeting to report on the progress of the garden and to make decisions about any new ideas that were raised. When a suggestion was agreed upon in the meeting, it became my job to find the curriculum links and that, surprisingly, was not difficult. For example, the running of a raffle to raise funds to purchase more plants was an opportunity to teach the concepts of profit and loss, money counting and probability. On another occasion, they ordered three cubic metres of soil. Lessons in 'volume' followed and they had the chance to see the quantity in reality. The lessons of the practical world were always there for the taking, not just in mathematics. No subject of the curriculum was without some reference to the garden, which meant planning was never easier.

By the end of the year, the food forest had spread over 1,000 square metres of the schoolyard and the children ran a field day to showcase their accomplishments. This was a time to write reports, practise speaking skills and learn how to host an occasion. It was also the time for me to reflect on what had happened that year.

Food Forest as a Revelation

The children's food forest was a revelation to me on many levels. I saw children at their best, working co-operatively on a project of their own design, using skills that they had to learn, in a place that was improved in the process. This was their path of discovery.

I was working at my best as well. I let the children take the lead and that worked for all of us. Daily planning became a joint effort that flowed with an ease that I had not found by working alone. We worked in the garden, but more often in the classroom, learning the content of the curriculum as it was revealed by the needs of the garden.

The children were totally engaged in the learning process, the community watched with pride and at the end of the project we were fulfilled by our efforts. A particular satisfaction was to see a child who had no success in the regular classroom blossom in this one.

We had demonstrated the power of a simple garden to be a successful setting for teaching and learning. By placing the learners at the centre of the curriculum, in a location that they were able to shape through an engagement of all their faculties; physical, intellectual and emotional, by using a hands-on experiential learning process, the children found success in things that went beyond the usual expectations of end of term tests. They took hold of their own learning, their school life and demonstrated their ability to do it in co-operation with their teacher.

This was a personally gratifying outcome and in the few years that I had in the children's food forest before my retirement, I was never more content with a process.

Not Just Gardens

A garden is one setting among many that could be set up for children to be engaged in the experiential learning process.

The key to success lies in the empowerment of the child rather than the setting. As wonderful as the garden is for this style of learning, there will be other settings that will inspire children and teachers accordingly.

Read Janet's story about how she became inspired.

Part II

A bit of background
Starting a school garden
Managing learning in the outdoors
School gardens and permaculture
Garden use is garden maintenance

A Bit of Background

I have had a very long and happy professional relationship with school gardens. My first school, Picnic Point Primary in Metropolitan South West Sydney, was rather new and the grounds very sparse when I arrived. So back in 1970 my supervisor, deputy, mentor and dear friend Harry Halpin and I used to get stuck into the garden with the kids whenever we had the chance. I would back up my old R4 full of tools and the boys would grab them out and we would get into it before school, lunch times or on sports days if the paddock was too wet for games. They were great times and it always amazed me how the kids who had the most difficulty inside were the greatest assets in the yard.

In those days the Gould League was the shining light of environmental awareness and one teacher needed to be the league's contact. I got the job, being the new teacher and needing to pull my weight. I think they thought I couldn't do too much harm with the environmental 'portfolio'. And so began my environmental activism in schools and I loved it. The kids loved it too and the gardens I started or enhanced are largely still there.

At Picnic Point we established small gardens in the quadrangle, planted trees for shade in the back paddock, and my greatest triumph was the establishment of the school forest. There was a rather significant stand of trees left between buildings and I went ahead with the boys and some parents clearing out the non-native intruders, then set about identifying and labeling all the trees without any botanical knowledge of native tree species myself.

At that time Allen Strom was making a name for himself as an environmental consultant to schools and I rang to ask him to come and identify our trees.

Allen was a striking figure arriving in his big black gum boots and green well-loved sweater. He walked around rattling off botanical and common names, which I obediently recorded. Allen was impressed with the trees that had been left and so were we.

The forest meant a lot to all of us and I was especially touched one day in 1973 when a very upset Jimmy brought his dead pet canary to school in a shoe-box to bury in our forest. We made quite a tribute, with the girls picking flowers and some of the boys helping Jimmy pen a fitting farewell to the poor bird. We had the service at lunchtime and all seemed fine until I found Jimmy in the forest after school digging up the bird. When I asked him what he was doing he explained that everything was alright, he was taking it home with him and would bring it back in the morning. I realised he had no idea of the finality of death or how the decomposition process would proceed.

Many things like that have happened in my 22 years in primary classrooms, it is just that first one that sticks in my mind so well as it was my first real glimpse back into the realm of childhood beliefs. It made me remember when I didn't know about death being the other side of life and when I didn't understand the processes that affect everything and everyone. I wondered how I had come to learn and why they were not painful lessons and I remembered all the days in the garden with my father. All the discoveries and talking about the real world and how things were, watching the passing of the seasons, eating from our garden, sharing produce up and down the street, these were the big lessons in life and I had learned them so easily in the garden.

So gardens have remained part of my life. Juggling them with the pressures of the curricula, time, planning and preparation and logistics meant that I didn't use them to the full. Today I believe they are even more important than ever and so I now work with schools to design, establish and maintain gardens and to integrate them with classroom work.

I have written the answers to all the questions and problems posed to me by teachers over the past three years. I have made a step-by-step guide to starting the garden project through to building the garden.

I have solutions for the garden maintenance throughout the year and during holidays. The chapter I most like is the one that shows how we can link the garden to all the learning that happens inside. My unit template makes programming easy and shows the full potential of working in or about the garden.

I hope you find my work useful and that you gain the same joy and satisfaction teaching in a garden as I always have.

Janet

Starting a School Garden

For the best results in a school garden or learning adventure installation, planning should begin well before the first sod is turned.

There is nothing difficult about building a garden. It can be done in less than a day with the right resources and help. The real challenge is to build something that is used to the full and maintained. In fact the more it is incorporated into the learning programs of the school the better are its chances of being maintained.

A well-designed and successful garden has a better chance of being used, so the design process must begin early. The garden must be a successful area of production, be aesthetically pleasing, be easily maintained without unreasonable use of resources and it must have strong links to all areas of learning activity within the school. So begin, not in the physical space of the school, but in the invisible systems and networks.

Any educational resource can only become a learning tool when it has links to the curriculum and to what is going on from day to day in the classroom. So before anything is built, the need for it has to be perceived by more than one individual or group in a school community. Whether you are doing this alone or with a motivated group you need to:

Gain Wider Support for the Garden

Initiatives always begin with a champion:

- find someone committed to outdoor learn-ing within the school community to drive the process
- form a core group of supporters and bring them up to speed
- undertake school community consultation
- share all information and skills

🐦 Once the idea begins to 'have legs', discuss the idea with teachers. This is a good time to bring in teachers from schools that already offer outdoor learning opportunities to talk about the benefits to their school.

Looking at real working examples is the best way to fast track the process. Teachers are always concerned about how much preparation and lesson time could be lost in a new approach.

Principals are often concerned about sinking human and financial resources into something that may become a maintenance problem in the future. So show them some real working examples and listen to teachers who have found the garden beneficial.

Below are exerts from a speech made by Claire Cox, School Community Involvement Officer at Palmwoods State School on the Sunshine Coast of Queensland, when accepting a community award for the school garden.

Working with students in the school permaculture garden has been a real inspiration …

I thought it would be difficult to engage children in the slow, quiet world of an organic vegetable garden, I thought they would become quickly bored and restless if things didn't happen fast enough. I took a deep breath before starting out in this journey, told myself I would have to be exceptionally patient, that they eventually would learn something even if it was only to be polite and show respect to the volunteers who came to help.

I am happy to say, I have been proven wrong on all counts – that my nerves and lack of confidence were no match for the zest and enthusiasm of young children given a new tangible project and a promise of watch and wait.

The REALNESS factor of a garden is the ultimate deciding factor in the usefulness of a permaculture vegetable garden in a school setting. So many children today are growing up without the time or mentoring that it takes to become knowledgeable and aware of how natural systems operate.

A well planned school garden program can give visibility to the words that are spoken in classrooms, on websites, in books about our environment, our health and our communities. Children can feel it, see it, smell it, hear it, taste it, do it and know it together and all in one go!

The students surprise themselves (and us) every week with what they know. They learn to care for the environment, the soil, the water and the plants. They learn to recycle, to make compost, to build up the nutrition and health of the soil. They learn to turn everything in the garden that is unwanted into a useful thing that helps something or someone else.

In a few short weeks, they learn that endless varieties of real food that you can eat, share with friends, that tastes wonderful and that costs only regular care and regular planning can grow in their garden. And it really happens!

Claire Cox

Later, other stakeholders may be brought into the discussions and they really should include members of the P & C and relevant community group leaders. Once your support group is formed you can discuss and prioritise the range of experiences to be offered to the children.

Only now can you even begin to think about creating the garden as a physical reality.

Bring in the Kids

This is perhaps the time to introduce the idea to the children. After all, the real success of the garden will be its ability to engage the kids. So giving them input and ownership of the project will ensure a high level of interest and enthusiasm that may carry the project forward and involve even the reluctant and the doubting in the school community.

Plan for a Whole School Gardening Project

1. **Raise the subject at a staff meeting to gauge the level of support**
   ✷ This will give you an idea about who will be involved, the scale of the first project and how to stage the vision.

2. **Present the concept**
   ✷ Present your idea to the school P & C and work with them to present the idea to the whole school community.
   ✷ An article in the school newsletter or a letter to parents is a way forward. It may surprise you just how much knowledge and materials are at hand.

3. **Involve the grounds staff**
   ✷ Remember the outdoors has been their domain almost exclusively. Many of the grounds staff will enjoy the new interest and activity while others give over exclusive authority ever so reluctantly. Diplomacy is necessary here as is giving respect to those who have worked in the grounds for some time and often with little recognition.

If co-operation comes too slowly, then the principal should point out the educational value of the outdoors as part of the educational programs offered and override any attempt to keep the school community out of the garden.

4. **Set up the steering committee and develop a design brief**
   ✷ So what do you want? It is time now to narrow it down and begin the wish list.

Where to Begin?

Usually the first components built are the herb and vegetable gardens. Starting here gives the opportunity to start small, gain a product and tap into education department initiatives that attract funding such as programs to address obesity, healthy eating, water conservation and discipline. And it is here, in the veggie patch where teachers and children can learn their gardening skills together.

The benefits of herb and vegetable gardens are:
✷ Creating places of observation. Growth, development (lifecycles), seasons, different solutions for similar objectives, systems thinking, diversity, interdependence, co-operation and niches in nature.
✷ Opportunities for outdoor activities where learning is valid. Providing hands-on activities to balance classroom activities, catering for all learning styles and addressing all eight of Howard Gardner's Multiple Intelligence Domains.
✷ Opportunity to increase physical activity and fitness. To create a lifelong interest in gardening as a leisure time activity or a possible employment opportunity.
✷ Increase awareness of methods of producing clean and healthy foods supports a healthy eating program.
✷ Provide an external model of the 'healthy in – healthy out' principle. Again supporting a healthy eating program.
✷ Encourage a sense of achievement through child-centered approach where students take ownership of the task and the outcomes. Supports Glasser's Quality Schools approach.

Ensure Links to the Curriculum

Good intentions and hope will not make school gardens a learning tool. Well-intentioned garden builders can wear out and their work may be lost without the connection to classroom learning activities and the community. This important area is discussed in depth in later chapters and examples are provided.

Possible Obstacles and How to Overcome Them

Once links to all learning programs are made, then identifying and pre-empting possible obstacles is the very next step.

1. **Leaving the Classroom**

    From my observation of many schools and my own teaching experience, it is moving out from the security of the classroom that causes the most resistance from teachers.

Solution: The Outdoor Shelter

Providing an outdoor learning centre, hub or shelter shed, is one way to move classes outside where gardens can be set up so that children move between the class work and the garden work in a way that allows for an easy transition from the confines of a classroom to the freedom of the outdoors.

The other alternative is to start small gardens beside the classroom or grow in pots and hanging baskets on verandas. The section on Managing Learning in the Outdoors will give detail and support to this concern.

2. **Teachers Feel Uncertain of Their Own Gardening Skills and Knowledge**

    At this point many teachers become nervous about their own knowledge and ability to grow a garden.

It would be wise to contact a permaculture practitioner at this point (on the staff or in the community) who can do a sector analysis and a zonal plan that considers resource and water catchment, storage and movement and who can plan for the needs of the children and staff in the master plan (see page 50, School Gardens and Permaculture). These experts may also lead the children through the design and establishment phases and beyond.

The following are things to consider in the design plan:

◎ Have a master plan (the tool box).

◎ Design and place one component of outdoor learning at a time.

◎ Always design maintenance into the system.

◎ Maximise learning experience from each component before planning and implement -ing the next.

◎ Involve all stakeholders.

◎ Consider functional aesthetics. (Things that work, are usually attractive and attractive things usually work.)

Solution: Teachers as Facilitators

Teachers only need to be one jump ahead of the children through reading some very simple books, watching one of the 'How to' DVDs or participate in workshops. They can acknowledge their lack of confidence and bring in a community member or enlist a student who is able to grow herbs and vegetables. All of these solutions have some merit and how schools manage this issue will depend on their own specific situation.

3. Designing the Garden so it Works

Finding the best place for the garden is a site-specific decision. Teachers rarely have the expertise or the time to design the garden, do the costings, develop a project budget, engage helpers, arrange deliveries, document the project and organise celebrations of important milestones.

Solution: Make the Project a Classroom Activity and Bring in the Experience

The children themselves can do a lot of the research and design work if supported by an 'expert'.

4. Lack of Funding

Schools have many projects going at any one time and there are always budgeting demands.

Solution: Apply for Grants and Start Small or Stage the Project

◎ If the garden can be used in any program for which there is government or even private funding, then the set up can be funded.

◎ Any time in this design phase, the garden project may be halted, to be revisited when support or funding becomes available.

◎ Schools can proceed without funding, as setting up a small successful garden is not expensive and can give an idea of the potential for a larger system or learning adventures.

5. Using the Garden to its Optimum Potential

Often the garden begins with one or a few interested teachers and participating classes. There is so much potential for learning, even in a small garden, that it seems a shame if it is not utilised by the whole school.

Solution: Relax. Teachers Will Notice the Work and the Potential

If it is happening too slowly, find as many links possible to the curriculum for each garden component and create units of work incorporating them. Do this for one before extending or taking on another garden challenge. Nothing succeeds like success and it is the links that keep the garden strong. So start small and consolidate in the garden and in the preparation of good lessons. Design tight units which support other curriculum areas.

6. The Challenges of Taking the Whole Class Outside

There are restrictions to taking a whole class group outdoors to all work in a small garden area.

Solution: Not Everyone Has to Work on Gardening

Other learning activities can be taken outside and groups may rotate one or several times during an outdoor session. The work may include:

- observational drawing or artwork
- reading silently or to a small group
- some measurement or calculations involving the garden and planning
- journaling and creative writing

Places for this work need to be close to the garden space so that the children are still well supported and supervised.

The outdoor shelter, seating under shady trees, some area of soft grass are all assets to the garden and allow the whole class to be outside at the one time.

Having volunteer or peer support may be another option depending on the whole school context.

7. Too Many Classes Want to Use the Garden at the One Time

Then of course the garden may be in high demand and may need to be shared or extended.

Solution: Have a Roster and Add Components

The rotations may be as short as a session or as long as a term. As each group will have a different focus, sharing can be as effective as your internal communications and booking system.

- Having a whole school plan will streamline this process even further.
- By adding components, children will have the opportunity to do a variety of activities and/ or have all the class outside at the one time. You will be able to get support for these from School Garden and Community Garden Networks, experts within the school community or simple garden texts. Some of these components are described in our section 'School Gardens and Permaculture' and may include:

a. worm farms

b. composting area

c. propagation shed

d. green house

e. extended gardens for broader crops such as pumpkins, sweet potatoes or cassava

f. various garden configurations such as raised beds, mandala gardens or keyhole gardens

g. orchard

h. animal systems

i. water garden or aquaculture production area

j. or any of the learning adventure installations

Supporters of Outdoor Learning Programs

Parents and other community members are valuable contributors in the establishment and maintenance of the learning space as well as in the development and presentation of learning activities in the outdoors.

When a volunteer sees the value of these learning environments they quite often will lend their time to support the concept. Roles will vary with the time availability, ability and confidence of the volunteer. Some will help maintain the physical resources while others will want to work with the children.

If you are a volunteer, or if you are a teacher who has volunteers, then this section will be of interest to you.

Volunteers

Volunteers play an important role in our schools. Many activities in the school day would not proceed without the assistance of the volunteer. The school community reaps the benefit of this freely given assistance and every effort should be made to encourage and support volunteer workers.

Volunteer – Assistant

These are parents, grandparents or community members who wish to support school programs and the classroom teacher. They are responding to a request for support in programs designed by teachers that are already running in a school.

Volunteer assistants may help in the classroom, on an excursion or in the canteen, but essentially they are supporting an established program. They generally are welcomed into an ongoing program by participating in some sort of induction process.

It is important that children understand that the role of volunteers is a giving and caring role and that they are demonstrating a valuable ethic in our culture. Children should not be dismissive of any person who offers to help. Teachers need to raise this awareness among the young and role model good behaviour towards volunteers themselves.

When a teacher shows respect to a volunteer, they are making a statement to the children and the visitor that the trust and respect earned by the teacher is being transferred in some part to the volunteer. Volunteers who are not 'endorsed' in this way by the teacher and/ or the principal, will have a much harder and less rewarding experience until they can earn the respect of the children for themselves. The opportunity to fast track the transfer of trust and respect should never be missed as it enhances the opportunity for learning and increases the job satisfaction for the volunteer, which is their only reward and ensures their return.

Volunteer – Initiator

Volunteers may come with an idea, a passion or an agenda. They may wish to support an aspect of learning that they feel is not being addressed, or addressed to the full, by the school. They are usually aware of the time limitations of teachers and volunteer their ideas and time in order to increase opportunities for the children and not to be critical of the school. In fact, volunteers who suggest new initiates are demonstrating a comfortable and healthy relationship with the school as an accepted part of the wider community. They trust that their ideas will be listened to and respected.

The volunteers, who have initiated the building of many food gardens in recent and not so recent times, are often graduates of permaculture courses or keen organic growers, and they are highly motivated to add gardening to the range of learning opportunities available for the children in the school.

They value teacher support, but in many cases, volunteer-initiators proceed with only the nod of the principal. Their resolve is to make a start and to grow the interest in the project and hope the benefits become visible.

Volunteer-initiators are well aware of the pressures of the curriculum and realise that the workload constraints on teachers means that the teacher cannot plan, deliver, assess, evaluate and report on learning experiences as well as build and maintain outdoor learning resources.

If your school is utilizing the services of a volunteer or a volunteer-initiator then the following are ways to gain maximum benefit from the relationship.

Look for a Win-Win Situation

Volunteers are very often prepared to establish gardens and work on their upkeep. Even small areas can be beneficial to learning across many learning areas. If the initial trial plots are small and reversible, then the only constraint may be the relationships between the teaching staff, the parent volunteers and curricula demands.

Many schools are embracing the school garden concept and are finding that all aspects of the school community benefits.

The most common model appears to be that:

1. A parent or teacher initiates a school garden, which becomes successful in a small area.

2. Later, other parents and teachers see the value of the learning space and the gardens expand and develop further on other sites within the school grounds.

3. Teachers begin to link the gardens with areas of the curriculum and then benefits begin to increase and the teachers share ideas.

4. As children progress through the school, teachers find further benefits of outdoor learning and begin to plan and document so that the garden will continue even through staff changes.

5. The garden becomes a focal point for the community and school interaction and innovative programs beyond the garden emerge.

6. Children gain the necessary learning response outside the confines of the classroom and teachers plan and utilise more outdoor learning adventure installations.

So many things happen when children are encouraged to learn beyond the walls of the classroom. It can happen more easily with the support and energy of a valuable community resource – the volunteer. Encourage them into your school garden.

How to Engage and Keep a Volunteer

Volunteers could be school supporters for just a few months or for many years. Parents at your school may have a family that will take from 7 to 15 years to pass through. I have even had parents continue to volunteer well after their children have left the school. By creating the opportunity for volunteers to engage with the school in presenting a diverse range of learning experiences, parents can adjust their commitment according to the time available, their family situation and their interest, skills and experience levels.

I have seen very successful programs run in schools without volunteers in the past. But it seems more and more to be the case that smaller learning group numbers are needed to create the optimum potential for learning.

If you do want to use volunteers, and especially in the garden, here are some suggestions that I have seen work:

1. Listen to their ideas and give them feedback as to the how their vision meets the reality of the working school.

2. Invite them to participate in planning sessions of programs that need the support of volunteers.

3. Ensure the volunteer is shown courtesy and respect from the entire staff and the children.

4. Have regular induction and updating sessions for volunteers.

5. Produce and update manuals for the various programs. (The volunteers themselves may be able to do much of this.)

6. Celebrate the milestones of programs with the volunteers. This can be achieved through a variety of activities such as morning teas, luncheons or even social evenings and bus trips. These will ensure each volunteer feels like a valued member of a vital team.

7. Invite well experienced local gardeners to provide a workshop environment. Volunteers love to learn and will work willingly if they go home with knowledge and perhaps some garden produce.

Managing Learning in the Outdoors

Class management in outdoor spaces is only now being identified as a distinct teaching challenge by teachers wanting to engage children in outside learning experiences.

Why do we need to manage learning in the outdoors? Isn't it natural for children to play and learn outside?

The relationship between humans and their environment has changed significantly, especially over the past 50 years. Even from the beginning of white settlement in Australia, the environment was seen as hostile, full of dangers and climatic extremes.

There have always been groups and individuals who have embraced the challenges of our great land, who have lived with it and loved it. Our traditional aboriginal people give us the best example of those who have gained the knowledge and skills to work with, rather than against nature, but in general it has been the aim of European settlers to control and dominate their environment. Early in our history we tried to make it look and behave like the 'homeland'. We have demanded the products that our culture expected.

We have divided the landscape with fences, roads and railways that interrupt natural flows and we have assumed the soils were formed, therefore would act, in the same way as those on other continents. These false assumptions have led to the slow deterioration of our environment and the increasing move of people from the bush into the growing towns and cities on our coastline.

Today many children see the environment as something they travel through to get from a home, with increasingly reduced back yards, to the place where they will do the 'real' things in life; working in classrooms, playing on sporting fields, swimming in concrete pools or shopping in malls.

As cities grow, natural areas shrink or are less and less accessible to children so that even a weekend visit requires careful planning and travel with parents. As work pressures increase for both parents, then short breaks become more difficult and as fuel prices rise, families choose to spend more time and money at home. So big screen TVs become a window to the world and computer experiences replace interaction in the real natural world.

Is taking children outside an unnecessary risk?

The built environment is so modified for our modern fast-paced lifestyle that most pavements are regular or flat, steps are a measured regulation size and height, any rough patches that may lead to litigation are smoothed while plants are selected and groomed with human safety in mind. In such a controlled environment, even being outside means that young and growing children do not develop ankle strength, the skills to pick a way across irregular ground, or in short, an ability to navigate the natural world without tripping or falling.

Children raised in a controlled environment have no understanding of dangers associated with how much load branches, rocks or other possible natural platforms, can support. They take the laws of the built environment into the outdoors, but there, structures are irregular and adhere to the natural laws that have not yet been explored or understood. Increasingly, as these skills and strengths are less developed any stumble does result in injury. Weak ankles sprain or break, falls create shock so carers and planners go to even greater lengths to make the environment 'safe'. This is done in the name of 'reducing risk'.

Is uneven ground the new level playing field?

Unfortunately if we do not provide our children with places to experience the natural world in their formative years, while their bones are young and quickly mended, while they develop muscles and an understanding of the qualities and behaviour of natural materials, we are actually putting them at even greater risk in later years as well as minimizing their potential for enjoying and respecting nature.

Many educators have among their charges, children who are 'at risk' from the natural world. Those children who have not developed the skills or understandings that were taken for granted even just 20 years ago. Educators will also have the responsibility for children who respond to being in the outdoors differently because of their home and family background as well as the messages the school may have given in previous years as to the value or possibility of learning in the outdoors. It is therefore important to start taking children outside for lessons from the beginning and to continue throughout their schooling.

This is possible by making meaningful educational connections between the classroom work and outdoor studies and is facilitated by children who have the ability to focus on tasks while outside.

Sometimes in the same group there will be children who have good knowledge and skills in working in nature. So along with children for whom being 'released' into the outside triggers a sense of free-for-all, resulting in characteristic running to the most obvious physical boundary or clambering up the nearest tree, a teacher will also need to cater for those who have good understanding of nature and who will value the opportunity to interact, observe and learn in the outdoors.

This need to cater for individual differences and working with heterogeneous groups is nothing new to educators. We anticipate that development across all learning areas will occur at different ages and rates.

It is just that we have always expected children to be able to operate in the natural environment 'like children' with innate dexterity, suppleness and enthusiasm. Today we can no longer make this assumption, as it is simply not the case.

Ready, Steady, Go Outside

Are we ready?

Taking children from behind a desk to participate in relevant outdoor activities needs to be carefully monitored by the facilitator. The release of the physical constraint of space may be seen as extending the rings of student responsibility for appropriate behaviour and learning, in ever expanding physical areas. It is also the transfer of control of the learning task and methods, from the teacher, to the student.

In the classroom the child has defined boundaries and the expectations are clear. But once part or

all of the class moves beyond the classroom walls, roles and responsibilities begin to shift. Over the time of formalized education, many teaching styles, methods and pedagogy, no matter what the philosophical or educational fashion, has contributed to the belief that the classroom is the principal place of learning. Since the industrial revolution many, if not most schools have seen themselves and their classrooms as the *only* place of learning.

The school grounds have been considered merely as a site on which buildings stand and places to which the children long to escape. The need was not so great in previous generations to include studies in or about the outdoors and natural phenomena, as the children were surrounded by them all the remaining hours of their days and weeks. But this is no longer so. Many children in our modern society rarely truly interact with their environment. They may run over it, move through it but they do not study it, observe it, ask it for a product, nurture or repair it. They don't listen for its calls or read the weather in the clouds or movement of birds. They hardly notice the passing of seasons and what produce each season might bring to their table. They recoil from anything creepy, crawly or slimy and have no idea the contribution to life of all but the cutest furry animals.

Once outside the door of the classroom, many of the deep cultural beliefs about place and learning trigger a 'caged bird' response and all social contracts are off. Inside the teacher is boss but outside kids rule. Many children we take outside are at serious risk as they have no idea of the laws of nature and are therefore vulnerable. We can fence in our swimming pools but fencing nature is very difficult.

How can we ensure all children know and understand natural laws?

As educators we need to lead children to a wider understanding of outdoors and outdoor work now that the gap between expectation and reality of our children's knowledge of nature and natural processes has become so noticeable.

This comes at a time when new curricula demand authentic experiences to make learning more relevant and to keep students engaged in learning and so gives us an opportunity and impetus to embark on new learning adventures outdoors.

Can the problem be the solution?

We now need to address the potential of the school grounds as a place where valuable lessons can be learned, not just about nature and growing, but about team work and observation, about systems thinking and job satisfaction, about a relationship with the elements that support us all and a joy and wonder more real and long lived than the latest computer game.

Greater interaction with components in school grounds can address the growing problems of child obesity and depression. Participating in school vegetable patches can develop healthy eating habits as well as self-reliance. Outside learning activities can show the possiblity of being sustainable and contributing to a better world and in so doing, empower the citizens of the future to improve their quality of life, even as our access to energy sources diminish. Beyond that, the learning adventure spaces can stimulate an interest or passion in one or more areas of study that will engage students who may not otherwise relate to class work.

To do this we need to gradually extend the physical barriers of the classroom walls and move children outside, taking with them all the same principles of sound learning practices that occur in a well managed classroom.

Imagine five learning zones in a school precinct. Spatially these zones move out from the classroom to the furthest boundary of the schoolyard. But these zones are not purely spatial; they are also described by the level of direction and supervision provided by the teacher. So out in Zone 5 the activity is purely child centred and child directed even if the physical space is right beside a classroom.

If the areas in which the child is to operate and the levels of direction and supervision are thought of as zones, then the first zone is the classroom.

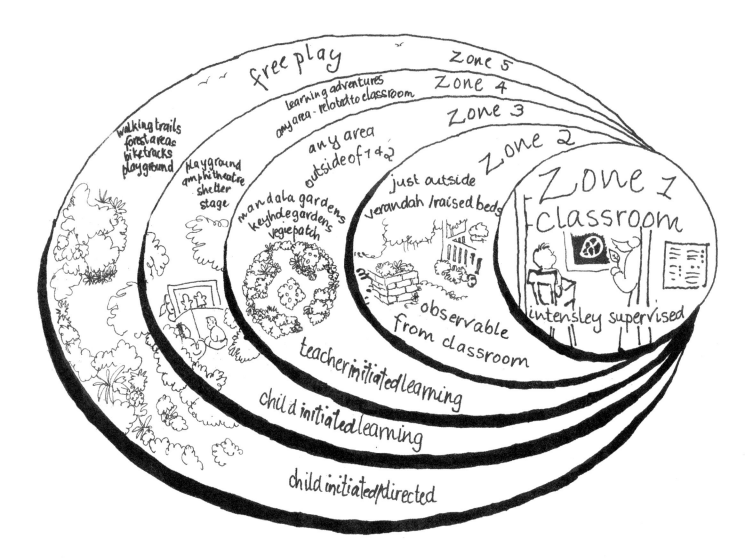

Free play — Zone 5
walking trails
forest areas
bike tracks
playground

learning adventures
any area - relate to classroom — Zone 4

playground
amphitheatre
shelter
stage

any area
outside of 1 & 2 — Zone 3

mandala gardens
keyhole gardens
vegie patch

just outside — Zone 2
verandah / raised beds

observable from classroom

Zone 1
classroom
intensley supervised

teacher initiated learning

child initiated learning

child initiated/directed

Zone 1 The Classroom

Classroom management is already the subject of many fine books and well covered in teacher training courses. The same management skills are used in outdoor lessons but the distinction between recreational breaks outside and *learning* outside needs to be clearly drawn in the minds of the children.

Switching on the learning brain in the outdoors is a wonderful ability and a skill that will benefit and reward the learner for a lifetime.

One approach is to use the learning model of the classroom and transfer that to outside activities. Teachers are usually comfortable with this as it is a natural extension of their own teaching style and it creates a seamless movement from indoors to outdoors for the children.

A Basic Classroom Management Checklist

A classroom management model will include the following:

Prior to the Lesson

- the lesson is well prepared
- the abilities and the behaviour patterns of the children are known and understood
- an explanation of the following 10 points is given to the children

1. **The boundaries of the workplace**

   Teachers need to make clear what sort of movement is appropriate for a particular task and how far they can go in physical space. The ability to vary this movement gives relief to monotony and allows some activity to stimulate circulation.

2. **Time limitations**

   The children must be given some sort of expectation as to the duration of the activity.

3. **Understanding of the task**

   The children must be made aware of the result or the product as well as the processes and tools used to gain the desired outcome. Generally a model is shown, a demonstration given, a set of instructions is provided or the steps have already been practiced.

4. **A sense of responsibility**

   Children are reminded about their responsibility to work in a manner that does not interfere with other learners in their room or adjacent rooms. They are also asked to take responsibility for the workplace and tools as well as making sure they clean up any mess and return equipment to the correct places.

5. **Risk assessment**

   Any dangers are pointed out to the children. In the classroom this may be in regard to the use of scissors or of electrical cords, or of the slippery floor and so on. The potential risks are minimized, removed or closely supervised.

6. **Pointing out special challenges that the task may involve**

   This may be those little tips, warnings or information that may stop a mistake before it is made.

7. **The consequences**

   All the participants should be made aware of the consequences of their actions and the way they go about completing the activity, in a well managed classroom. This is generally well known to all and only needs restating on special occasions or when standards appear to be slipping.

8. **What to do if the task becomes too difficult or uncertain**

   This is when learners are asked to indicate if they are unsure or confused. When in the classroom, that may be a hand raised or a visit to the teacher or moving to a group that the teacher is working with. These contingency plans are usually well practiced when working with a familiar teacher in a classroom and only occasionally need to be varied or restated.

9. **What to do on completion of a task**

   Always start with the end in mind.
   How will the learner be sure the task is complete? When it is complete then what will they go on with while others catch up? And what will happen if time runs out and they don't finish?

10. **Feedback to the student**

   Feedback may be given during the task as well as on completion but it is very important to let the learner know they are on the right track as soon as possible. Making a correction as soon as an error is identified will ensure the incorrect response is not repeated and learned.

Following a lesson

The teacher deals with two more things that will impact on classroom management issues. These are assessment and evaluation, which are an integral part of the management loop.

Assessment

Assessment is well covered in teaching manuals and is mentioned here briefly so that it is considered just as seriously when the work is done outdoors. We need to be able to assess students as to the level of competency, but increasingly we need to assess many of the core competencies at the same time. These may be organisational skills, the ability to follow instructions, team-work and so forth.

Preparation of checklists that are easily ticked during an activity can help to identify learners who are achieving and those who, as yet, have not achieved a suitable standard or met a specific benchmark.

In many cases the activity and its outcomes are also the assessment tool. Supported by the observation checklist and possibly some worksheets, the doing can become the testing/ assessing.

Evaluation

Without critical appraisal of the teaching/ learning activities, their flexibility, validity and ability to enhance the learning for our students, we are unable to design or plan further successful activities.

Taking a good look at what has worked and what didn't, as well as listening to the suggestions from children, and seeing the cross-over to other Key Learning Areas, facilitates the design of more effective learning experiences in the future.

When can we extend the physical boundary of the classroom?

Management problems inside are always magnified once the physical boundaries are extended.

If all the management principles are not yet used effectively in the classroom, then do not take a group outside alone. It only takes a flaw in any of the management parameters to bring the lesson down and to set up an undesirable response when learning outside on future occasions.

Are there more benefits to moving lessons outdoors?

As we face an energy challenged future, we will need to ensure the comfort of children without air-conditioning. Outdoor classrooms, under shady trees are cool and breezy places that provide pleasant conditions for learning activities. The out-gassing of chemicals from fluorescent lights, plastic furniture, vinyl flooring or synthetic carpets in modern classrooms on hot days can affect health and brain function.

Zone 2

Zone 2 is the area adjacent to the classroom, which is visible to the teacher from inside the classroom and offers the children the opportunity to enjoy outdoor space while still adhering to the culture of the classroom.

Many modern classrooms are designed with these spaces in mind. Montessori Schools have always demanded them. Rooms can open onto a small courtyard for quiet reading, reflection or observation.

Group work can be undertaken in this outside space or teacher aides can work with children with specific needs away from the larger group.

Older schools often have verandah space or outside areas close to the classroom that can be utilised for a similar purpose. Perhaps they are already used as 'break-out' areas but they are also useful to take the whole class with a specific task in mind. It is an excellent place to practice moving the classroom management principles outside.

Here we are able to gradually extend the physical boundary while still adhering to the constraints of acceptable behaviour in a learning environment. This area is also a 'safe' place, well known to the child and any dangers will have been explained and or dealt with previously.

When designing whole-group outdoor learning experiences, ensure they are meaningful and relevant to the child and that they appear to the child as a natural extension of the classroom work. They should have an element of fun and should provide variety to the school day.

In the early stages, out-side visits can be short with follow up work, recording or discussion being completed back in the classroom. The key is that working outside is stimulating and adds to the quality of the classroom experiences.

Some examples of the sort of work that can be undertaken in Zone 2 are:

- setting up of experiments with controls and treatment components
- setting up measuring equipment such as a rain gauge or thermometer
- observational drawing
- collection of seeds
- growing herbs or creating a small vegetable garden
- measuring and counting activities of various kinds
- silent reading
- reading pairs/groups

Not only will you be creating variety, but the children will also gain the important skill of transferring behaviours and values from one context to another, therefore gaining skills to move into even larger learning spaces.

What if not all the children are ready?

Teacher aides and parent helpers may be necessary if a teacher feels the group may find the transition difficult and there is always the opportunity, in this close zone, to just pack up and go back into the classroom. This should always be a consequence known to the children. But it is necessary to carefully watch for the patterns of behaviour that trigger the 'back inside' consequence and address them without reinforcing them.

Remember that while outside, the children are no longer focused in the same direction; they become very involved in the new surroundings, they know that as an individual they are less visible to you, and your voice does not travel as well. To overcome this you may need a visual and/or aural signal.

Don't take a group outside until you have a signal that they will all respond to immediately and without question. You may have one for 'stop and listen' and another for 're-group'.

This response can be tried and tested during physical education classes or even in the room before you venture out. The aim is not to develop a pack of Pavlov's dogs but to ensure that once a group has dispersed into a wider environment that they can be called back when needed. This may be necessary because of a safety issue, a change in weather conditions, clarification of instructions or simply that time is up.

Zone 2, being within sight of the classroom and the work being an extension of the class work, is the best place to start. When you are sure your charges can operate safely and effectively there, then it is time to move into Zone 3.

Zone 3

Zone 3 is any area of the school grounds outside of Zones 1 and 2 designated by the teacher as a directed learning space.

Here the physical boundaries have been significantly extended and you may be close to, or even in, an area that is used for recreation at other times of the day. The site now has the potential to prompt the learned 'let's play' response. Without reducing the sense of adventure and fun, the teacher must manage the activity so as to switch on the learning brain in this playtime setting.

Addressing all the classroom management principles before and during this activity is crucial to its success.

Suggested Activities in Zone 3

- reading or listening to a story
- preparing, planting and maintaining gardens
- propagating
- sowing and collecting seeds
- making observations
- classifying and labelling
- drawing
- celebrating
- monitoring conditions

When children are completely secure in their ability to follow work processes in Zone 3, they are able to move outwards into Zone 4.

Zone 4

Zone 4 is any physical area of the school which is used by the student to observe, explore or interact with the real or natural world on a task related to classroom work but selected and designed by the child.

Zone 4 is the zone where the learning is child-centred and self-directed.

In a well designed school precinct, there should be a variety of opportunities for children to explore the real world with their own curiosity, skills and imagination and to participate in learning adventures.

As children become more familiar with using the outdoors they will start to make links between it and the inside lessons and they will begin to suggest activities or ask to test an hypothesis.

These sessions in Zone 4 will become increasingly meaningful to the learners with practice and should become a natural extension of the class work rather than a contrived activity to do outside.

In Zone 4 the teacher is there to support the child in their chosen work and to monitor safety or behavioural issues. Just as in all of the previous zones, the lesson must adhere to all the management principles and this child-centered learning must be as thoroughly prepared and monitored as any activity in all previous zones.

In Zone 4 the child directs the learning but the teacher supports with methodologies, tools and the consolidation of the vision of the outcome. Depending on whether the child starts with a question or a desired product or something else, the teacher can guide the child with suggested activities and outcomes when and if necessary.

As discussed earlier, the opportunities for children to participate in this very important learning activity are becoming less as our towns and cities grow, as dangers to children from other individuals and groups in society increase, as more time is given to organised recreational activities and as educational outcomes are measured quantitatively.

We are feeling the effect of the loss of this important factor in child development if only we can make that link between the symptoms and the underlying problem.

What are these symptoms?

Educators are aware of the increasing numbers of students who disengage from school and learning, the shortening attention span and lack of focus, increased aggression/bullying towards other students and teachers, inappropriate behaviour, depression, obesity, stress and other indicators of imbalance that were once rarely seen in children.

Is the underlying problem alienation from nature and the real world?

All the symptoms above can be addressed, to some extent, by children being able to apply knowledge and skills in the real world, in authentic and relevant situations selected and designed by them as the learner.

Are we seeing the consequences of a change in societal behaviour?

The out of school hours of my generation and even the generation of my, now adult children, were spent very differently to out of school time today. For many reasons, children have less free time, less interaction with the environment, even less time interacting in relationships with their peers, where they need to negotiate and plan what the 'game' will be.

Putting it another way, they have less opportunity to put the skills learned in the classroom to use, to set themselves challenges that utilise the skills and knowledge gained at school and to also identify, in the imagined or 'game' world, those skills that they will need to learn in order to be successful in the tangible world.

This fracture between the 'learning world' and the 'concrete school world' is often indicated by comments such as 'Why do I have to know this?', 'I will never need to know that, or the most common 'This is boring – these are the child's judgements of any activity that is meaningless to them.

Have we underestimated the huge impact of the access to virtual worlds offered to our children?

Computer games allow the player to interact with time, space and others in a way that is gratifying but not indicative of the constraints and consequences in the real world. The virtual game world allows for super-powers and release from physical boundaries. Running up walls and on ceilings is possible, amazing speeds can be reached and no consideration is necessary for other players, who can be hit or killed without justice or mercy and who will always be back for the next turn. It is little wonder that the incidence of childhood depression is escalating. The real world must seem such a disappointment and far removed from the learning tasks of the school. Disappointment can lead to anger and we see ever increasing incidents of bullying, violence and even murder in our learning institutions.

Suggested activities in Zone 4

- ☽ observing
- ☽ recording by drawing, photography, video and in words
- ☽ setting up small research projects using control and treatment areas
- ☽ designing and planting a small garden bed.
- ☽ estimating and measuring distances, structures and plants
- ☽ monitoring different aspects of climate and weather
- ☽ propagating
- ☽ seed gathering and sowing
- ☽ preparing presentations and demonstrations for classmates and/ or other class groups
- ☽ participating in different aspects of animal care
- ☽ conducting surveys and audits

If schools wish to mend the fracture between the learning world and the real world then they need to provide the spaces and the time for child directed learning outdoors. This does not mean less time for the 'important' subjects. It means more quality time for learning with fully engaged students and focused, meaningful time during recreational breaks in a stimulating environment where lessons meet imagination in healthy play.

This brings us to the 'playing' zone and the important concept of the Play Approach to Learning.

Zone 5

In Zone 5 children 'play' and use any of the physical areas permitted as recreational spaces. The only supervision is the regular playground-duty teacher.

Modern living has taken away many opportunities for children, but the one that is most significant in the development of cognitive skills, is the loss of practical application in the real world at the level of each child, in activities that are meaningful for each child.

Unfortunately it is impossible to return to the halcyon days when there was the freedom, the relative safety and the stimulating areas of nature for children to do this for themselves.

So it becomes yet another responsibility of the school to provide the space, the designed places for this essential part of child development and learning.

There is minimal teacher preparation required in this zone for these recreational breaks to be an effective educational tool. Exploration of an area in class time may open up some of the opportunities for a variety of uses of the space in free time. The space must be designed in such a way that several potential uses can be made of it.

To give a simple example here, a small deck may be used as a stage for a performance. It may be the deck of a ship or the last iceberg for a polar bear to cling to. How it is used would depend on whether the children are preparing for the school concert, had just studied the voyages of Captain Cook or had been introduced to the effects of Global Warming. Its use would also depend on the depth of feeling relating to an issue.

Along with children's art, this play period can give an insight into the joys, fears or confusion a child may have around an issue; be it a personal one regarding relationships or a global issue. Monitoring these sessions can give an early indication of a problem that may need addressing or a child that could need some support during a difficult time.

Generally it will be a place of imagination and testing of abilities, both physical and social.

Suggested activities for Zone 5

Free play

No suggested links between class work/ themes and different designed components in the playground.

Guided play

Teacher suggests play that may stem from class work and the particular designed component.

Supported play

Teacher may support the play by allowing children to use class resources in the outdoors such as an audio player or dress-ups.

Teacher gains insight

Supervising teachers can monitor the style of play, the feelings expressed and the ability to deal with issues and others. This knowledge can then be used to plan learning activities, that better address the learning and emotional needs of the children.

So how do we assess, evaluate and report outdoor learning outcomes?

As for inside work, assessment and reporting on outdoor learning follows the lesson. With some of the new educational guidelines, it is only this outdoor work that can provide the opportunities to guide and assess students in areas of key processes and values.

Evaluating the lesson will help refine the learning experiences in the future and will suggest further curricula links. Sound, validated evaluation will also provide a record that can be accessed by other teachers using the outdoor spaces and suggest the value of creating further outdoor learning adventures.

By increasing the opportunities for children to reinforce classroom learning in the outdoors, schools can enhance the understanding that comes from applying knowledge and skills in authentic and relevant situations.

So what does that all mean in a nutshell?

It is possible that by providing a school garden and other outdoor learning adventures that schools will be able to engage more children in the learning process and have the ability to address more of the broader areas of the curriculum.

Rather than being added work and responsibility for teachers, using well designed outdoor learning spaces may reduce behaviour problems, increase learning, reduce stress, increase health and wellbeing, increase links with the community and provide the means to assess the skills and knowledge delivered in the classroom.

In our attempt to prepare children to operate in the real world we need to lead them to true understanding of, and the ability to, interact with the outdoors.

Children's Roles and Responsibilities in the Outdoor Classroom

Many schools have codes of conduct for classrooms, play areas, toilet areas etc., and may need to upgrade these to show the continuity of behavioural expectations and special challenges in the school garden and the outdoor learning adventure installations.

Children need to be made aware that new or special rules apply when they work outdoors in a garden. Schools may choose to set up a code of conduct for the garden. Included below are some of the issues that we have identified as important for the safety and well-being of the children in the garden.

For Safety Know…

☽ The boundaries of the learning zone

☽ The signal to stop and the signal to re-group

☽ How to carry and use tools safely (Sharp ends down)

☽ How to work safely in pairs

☽ How to use the proper protective clothing such as covered shoes and hats

☽ The appropriate tool for each task

☽ Your physical capacities and limitations

☽ That the garden is an outdoor classroom

For Safety Do…

☽ Wear your protective equipment (hats, gloves, covered shoes)

☽ Use face masks and gloves when using potting mix or spreading hay or dealing with compost

☽ Act appropriately by working co-operatively and safely

☽ Take a water bottle to the garden in warm weather

☽ Walk on paths and move cautiously through the garden when others are working

☽ Return all garden equipment before leaving the garden

☽ Leave garden timbers and/ or rock edges in place

☽ Wash your hands when garden work is completed

☽ Stay in the designated areas

☽ Listen to instructions

☽ Be aware and observant at all times

Show Respect by...

- Co-operating with the teacher

- Approaching the teacher or supervisor to ask a question in a speaking voice

- Checking before undertaking an unfamiliar task or unsure of what to do

- Sharing equipment

- Moving on to next task when asked

- Showing team spirit in outdoor activities

- Speaking politely to all visitors

Learn best by...

- Being observant

- Looking for any changes in growth or decay

- Checking for plant and animal health

- Staying focused on the task

- Recording all observations and findings if asked

- Playing different roles in working groups

- Taking the skills learned in the classroom into the garden

- Taking the lessons learned and questions asked in the garden back to the classroom

School Gardens and Permaculture, or How to Build a Sustainable Garden

Permaculture techniques and strategies are ideal for establishing successful gardens in school grounds. With over 30 years of growing experience and thousands of trials in all climates, permaculture offers the best way to garden in compacted soils, using no chemicals, with minimum work, for the best results. Working with degraded soils and managing weeds and insect pests without poisons are significant challenges when working in school grounds. Along with them come the issues of extended periods of little or no care during holidays and limited access to water even during school times.

The permaculture principles for producing clean healthy food are working in school gardens throughout Australia and the world. Permaculture is based on three ethics: Care of Earth and Species, Care of People and the Return of Surplus to Earth, Species and People.

All Decisions are based on Ethics and Principles

These ethics cross all cultural and religious divides and provide an ethical basis for all decisions in the garden. These choices may be about growing food in a pot on a veranda, catching and storing water, managing areas of native bushland, housing and using animals, or the distribution of the produce.

Whatever the goal, demands or constraints, by basing decisions on the ethics and action on the principles, permaculture will deliver the best outcomes.

There are now two sets of principles as stated by both founders of permaculture. The first set comes from the design manual by Bill Mollison. Although many more principles are implicit in his text, usually 12 - 15 main principles are attributed to Bill. These are design principles or guiding statements that help to achieve the best results when designing, usually a garden, property or house but these universal design principles can be applied to any situation from agriculture through to business and relationships.

The second set of 12 principles has been devised by David Holmgren and these are more about universal situations and why or how to design and act. They are about the thinking or strategic principles rather than the more practice-oriented principles of Bill Mollison. These global principles are also more clearly and directly relevant to the way we plan for the reduced access to, and the effects of the burning of fossil fuels.

Bill Mollison's Principles

1. 'Enough' is the key principle of wise resource use.
2. Work with nature not against it.
3. The problem is the solution. *or* see solutions not problems.
4. Make the least change for the greatest possible effect.
5. The yield of a system is theoretically unlimited.
6. Everything gardens.
7. Everything works both ways.
8. Design to accelerate succession and evolution
9. Use relative location.
10. Each important function is supported by many elements (components).
11. Each element (component) performs many functions. *or* Use everything to its highest capacity.
12. Bring food production back to the cities.
13. Help make people self-reliant.
14. Increase diversity and so increase stability.
15. Co-operation not competition.

David Holmgren's Principles

1. Observe and interact.
2. Catch and store energy.
3. Obtain a yield.
4. Apply self-regulation and accept feedback.
5. Use and value renewable.
6. Produce no waste.
7. Design from pattern to detail.
8. Integrate rather than segregate.
9. Use small and slow solutions.
10. Use and value diversity.
11. Use edges and value the marginal.
12. Creatively use and respond to change.

Primary schools seem to be choosing to use the Holmgren principles as they easily apply across curricula, while the more specialist high schools use the Mollison principles in association with systems thinking, agriculture or horticulture.

There is no doubt that both sets are about permaculture and neither expresses all of the other. Each teacher should decide which principle/s fit with which topic or activity and use the ones that give the children the best tool for the task at hand.

A Design System

Permaculture is a design system and so, doing a whole school plan and positioning the design components in a way that gives the best outcomes for the least effort and producing the least waste, is the fundamental step. This design process should, as far as possible, contain every element a school is likely to need for outdoor learning. List and allocate positions to all features identified in your design plan then prioritise the projects. Areas to be developed later can be used to grow mulch for existing gardens or simply put under a cover crop to stop erosion and gain a yield.

Sector Planning

Your whole school design must take into account all the incoming energies. This first step is known as Sector Planning and requires the observation of all the energies coming to the proposed site. Look at the sun and heat sector, the cold or damaging winds, the hot summer winds and fire sector. Consider noise, views and anything else that will impact on the site. The idea is to place components so as to encourage the beneficial energies and to block or modify any negative influences. At this time the impact of water must also be considered to ensure the gardens won't flood and, at the same time, to ensure they can have and hold the water they require to be productive.

Zonal Analysis

Following the sector analysis, look at the energies of the people who will be working in the designed system. It is that energy, or lack of it, that will determine the size and placement of the components. The Zonal Analysis will show that places frequently visited should be positioned close to the 'home' or base in Zone 1 and from there the zones range out depending on the number of visits.

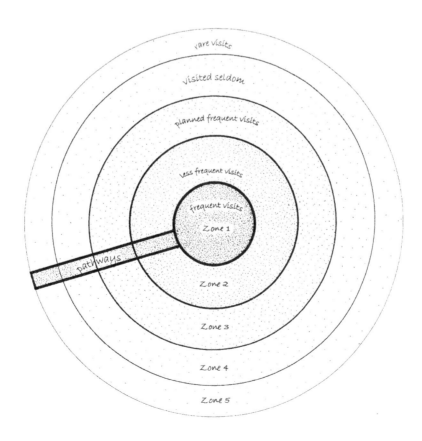

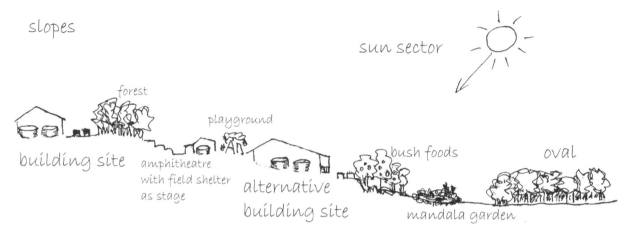

Slope diagram, based on the concept in *Permaculture Two* by Bill Mollison, page 19

Closer zones are for those things requiring frequent visits and distant zones are for infrequent visits. Zone 5 is the furthest zone where we do little work but where we go to observe natural systems and to perhaps enhance them.

Using Slope to Advantage

Next is the slope and aspect of the site or components in the plan. The ability to catch and store water is linked with the ability to work with slope. Slope can also affect the amount of sunlight and influence wind effect and air temperature. So by understanding and using slope we can move and store water, create shelter belts and thermal zones. Even a seemingly flat site has some slope that can be used. Or, with our terra-forming techniques, we can create slope that will increase the production or restoration capability of the site very quickly.

Increasing Edges

The use of the edge effect is an important consideration in all permaculture design. The edge is where two different media meet and can be the most productive place. Why is it that all the growth, planned and unplanned, occurs on the edge of pathways or beside water bodies? It is because of the diversity of niches at the boundary. The path collects water, seeds and nutrients, and directs them to the garden. It is a thermal mass that holds heat, it is low and allows the plants on the edge to have plenty of light and even receive reflected light and there is no

competition for nutrient, as the path takes nothing from the plant. Increasing the edge can also increase growing spaces and growing niches. Flat land can be increased by making mounds and ditches which create more planting spaces. These niches vary in the amount of sun, wind and water they receive depending on their position on the mound and will support a wide variety of species in a small area. This is why a permaculture garden may well have winding paths and mounds and can be stacked with a variety of plants rather than flat straight beds catering to a single or a few plant species.

Using Succession

Permaculture then has other design strategies which reduce work and increase productivity. An essential consideration for school gardens or forest establishment is designing for succession. The use of volunteer and pioneer species will create the right growing conditions and nurture the target species.

Even as the system develops, permaculture design requires a number of support species that will help the growth and production of the target species. These are most often legume plants that provide filtered light, mulch and nitrogen to the productive plants or trees.

Part of this same strategy is the planting design of a food forest that reflects the layers of a forest in nature. A forest has canopy, understorey, shrubs, herbs, ground covers, plants with underground food storages and vines. These layers interact with nutrients and light, while providing shelter and support so they can be more productive together than any would be alone.

To a lesser extent, we use the same strategy in our vegetable gardens as we stack them with many species. This is often referred to as 'companion planting' or 'creating guilds' and it is one of the more obvious visible signs that permaculture principles are being used in the garden. The mulching of the garden is also utilisation of this mimicry of natural growing systems and it fulfills the functions of the forest floor litter that reduces evaporation and increases nutrients while protecting the soil biota.

Vital Living Soils

The understanding of the living soil is an essential permaculture principle. Where water and nutrients are returned, the soil can then maintain high levels of soil biota, from small bacteria and fungi to bugs and worms that work to nourish the plants.

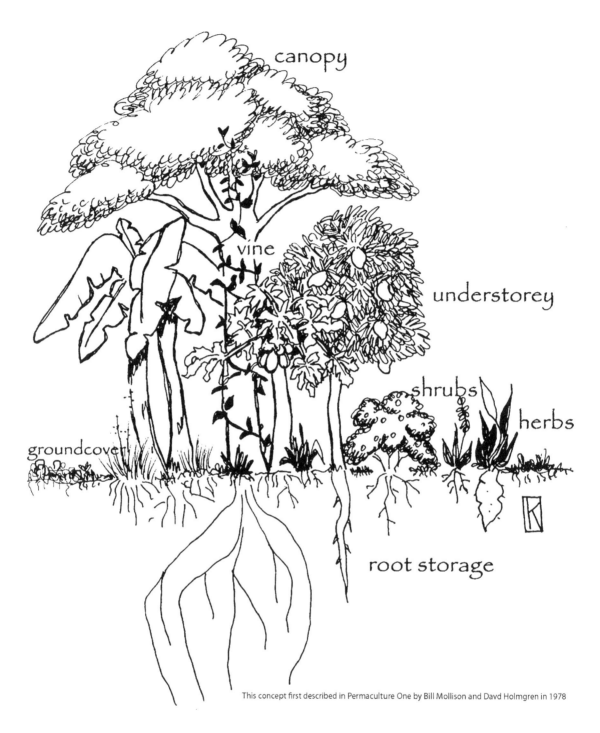

canopy

vine

understorey

shrubs

herbs

groundcover

root storage

This concept first described in Permaculture One by Bill Mollison and Davd Holmgren in 1978

No-dig gardens reflect the permaculture understanding of soil life and so this layered garden plays an important role in garden development and management in our designed systems. Raised gardens with their easy access and maintenance are a good example of many permaculture principles working together to get the best possible effect.

Systems Thinking

Permaculture gardens usually have compost heaps and/ or worm farms that return nutrients to the system that would otherwise be lost to the garden when food is harvested and taken away. While our human body system is an open one, requiring a constant flow of energy, in permaculture we try to create a closed system that utilises waste to return and circulate energy, water and nutrients between humans and their supporting systems. Permaculture design keeps all energy flowing so that there is less work and no waste thus making permanent agriculture and permanent human culture possible.

Permaculture does not want to change natural eco systems into food production and in fact emphasizes the need to keep and restore natural systems so they can provide the essential eco-services needed to maintain our Earth as a functioning living system. Some of these essential services are the cleaning, filtering and circulating of air and water, modifying the effects of heat, cold, storms, winds and the provision of habitat and essential parts of the nutrient cycle. There will be other services that are, at this point, beyond our understanding and whose function we may only come to know when they are lost. So permaculture has a deep reverence of natural systems and the wonders they are yet to reveal.

Putting Permaculture to Work in Your School

Permaculture gardens work in schools on a number of levels:

- they are easy to establish on compacted and degraded land
- once established they are easy to maintain and require no artificial chemical input
- they model sustainability principles
- they give children the opportunity to interact with a functioning system and so to develop systems thinking
- many community members know permaculture techniques and can support children and the staff in the garden
- permaculture has a global network that can link schools all over the world

Hopefully this very brief introduction to the possibilities permaculture design has for the success of the school garden, will stimulate further investigation. There are many excellent books on the subject and there will be active permaculture practitioners who will help you to get your garden going.

Maintenance of your vegetable garden, orchard, forest or any of the learning adventure installations is made easier by using permaculture. So start with a good design and use proven strategies to ensure the success and longevity of your school garden.

The Garden Components

The following steps are a guide to establishing garden components that although can stand alone, will be far more productive and a better model, if linked so that the placement ensures less work and no waste. If possible it is a good idea to involve the children in the decision-making process from the beginning so the teacher acts as the facilitator rather than the expert.

The No-Dig Garden

This is a classic component of a permaculture system and reflects the permaculture understandings of:

- working with nature not against it
- maintaining life in the soil by not turning it over and exposing it to the sun
- working with weeds and using them as dynamic accumulators of nutrient lost to the topsoil
- reflecting the lessons in nature in the forest floor litter

A No-Dig Garden is a useful technique in schools because they can;

- be established very quickly with little cost
- be removed or extended easily
- continue to be highly productive for years with no hard infrastructure at all

Once the garden site and how it will be watered is decided, then it is time to begin this layered garden first described in 'Ester Deans' Gardening Book: Growing Without Digging' (1977) and then well described in many permaculture texts.

The steps outlined by Robin Clayfield in her book 'You Can Have Your Permaculture and Eat it Too' (1996) is a clear and practical guide for beginners. The following is an adaptation.

Step 1 Select the site and don't worry about the number or vigour of weeds, as these will be cut to form a nutrient layer.

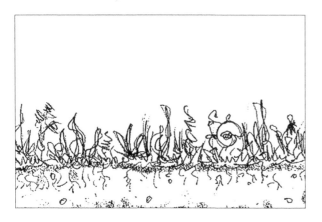

Step 2 Cut the weeds as low as possible. Sprinkle the area with anything that will balance the soil (check pH, if it is low add lime, if the soil is clayey add gypsum and always add manure, blood and bone or anything that will attract the attention of worms).

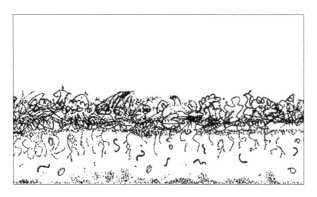

This is the rich nutrient layer that will feed the life in the soil and gain the attention of the small soil workers from all around. You can make it as rich as the resources available to you allow.

Step 3 This is the weed suppressant layer. Cover the area with a thick layer (at least 6 sheets and well overlapped) of wet newspaper. Tougher weeds require thicker layers; really pile it over woody weeds that may perforate the paper. If you do want to use cardboard put it under newspaper or old natural fabrics and never use it on a path that has any slope as it becomes very slippery when wet.

Give this layer a final water.

Some people are rightly concerned about the inks and dyes in print and fabric. It is best not to include glossy publications, but most inks are now vegetable based and many chemical chains are broken down by the alchemy of the worms and other soil biota. Worms are used in brown field clean ups and have been found to be effective in remediation of oil and petrol spills. So the more suspicious the materials, the more worm attractors you should add to your layers. If there are concerns at your school regarding the paper or cardboard, then the simple alternative, and one used for decades by permaculture practitioners who do no have access to paper or cardboard as a suppressive mulch, is to use broad leaf plants such as banana, arrowroot or palm fronds as the suppressive weed barrier. As long as it is thick, restricts light and breaks down slowly it will do the job. I have even used coconut husks for this layer. The beauty of permaculture is that you use what is available and what fits with what you know to be concerns or health issues.

Carpet has been used as a weed suppressant layer in the past, but I would avoid it because of the treatments it may have had and the addition of synthetic fibres into the warp or weft. These do not break down and end up as fine fibre strands throughout the garden. They are often selected by birds to be used as nest building materials and can twine around the small legs of babies in the nest, which results in painful crippling. So try to avoid carpet. But if you must, it can be useful under wood shavings or chips for paths and should be turned regularly then discarded when it begins to disintegrate.

Step 4 Add the carbon/ nutrient layer, which may be any manures, dried leaves, sawdust, straw or anything else you would use to make healthy compost. This layer should be about 5-8cm deep. The deeper and richer this compost layer, the more productive the garden will be for a longer time.

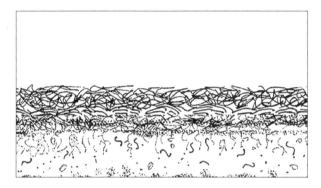

You may choose to add rock minerals here that will provide the slow release of minerals in a living soil over months or years.

Step 5 This is the mulching layer and should be at least 10cm but better up to 15cm thick. It could be hay or straw, sugar cane or bamboo leaves and it is added to suppress weeds that may volunteer into the top of your garden and to shade and shelter the plants, their roots and the soil. This layer can be supported by the planting choices around the garden bed. Boundary plants are selected to shade, be a weed seed barrier, shelter the plants from winds and provide materials that can be 'chopped and dropped' directly onto the garden.

Step 6 Water all the layers without saturating them. What you want is moisture and oxygen to begin the processes.

Step 7 Make a planting mix to plant into the mulch and compost layers. This mixture should hold moisture but also drain well as you will be planting above the soil and paper layers. Do not pierce the paper layer for 1-2 years (depending on the vigour of the weeds you covered). My preferred mix on clay soils, taught to me by Mark Fry, is a mixture of river sand, compost, worm casting manure and crusher dust. If your soil is already sandy you will need to add a little clay to this mix. Dissolve some clay in a bucket of water and add a little of this water to the mix.

This will help bind the minerals in the growing media. The proportions will depend on the water and nutrient needs of the plants and your climate. You will soon know when you get it wrong as the plants will wilt through lack of nutrient, sour soil or burnt roots, so try a few in your mixture a few days ahead of the main planting.

Step 8 Make holes in the mulch layer and fill with the planting mixture. Plant the seedlings or more mature plants. It is best not to try to raise plants from seed in the early seasons of your no-dig garden, but soon enough your heritage varieties will begin to self seed and you will be amazed at the growth that flourishes without you having to plant them out.

At that stage you will really only need to go in and thin out the over abundance.

Step 9   To maintain the garden will take just a few minutes every few days. In the early days the main thing to watch is the water as you are growing above the soil. Later when the layers sink, then the maintenance is governed by your planting strategy. At any time, some or all the garden can be put over to a cover crop that can be turned in or harvested and then composted. Or you can cut everything back, add a new compost layer/s, some worms, and a thick mulch layer, perhaps cover with hessian sacks or shade cloth and go on a six week holiday, in the heat of the summer. You will come back to a garden ready to plant in the new school year.

The Raised Garden, Earthring or Tank Garden

Raised garden beds in schools are useful because:

- They are at a working level for children who can use more of their limited, (depending on age) peripheral vision than when they have to look down. They actually get to see more of the garden, of the other children and more of the teacher.

- It is easier for a teacher to point something out to a number of children at the one time rather than just the front row when looking down to the ground.

- Working in an upright position is easier and causes less strain than bending.

- Pathways are easier to maintain if the garden is defined and raised.

- Fewer weed seeds from the path are transferred into a raised bed.

- They are very simple to 'close down' over holiday breaks or spells between class use. The same procedure as for No-Dig gardens step 9 turns them into cover crop areas or instant worm farms.

- They allow a garden to be placed in damp or possibly boggy places as they can drain well, being above ground.

Ester Dean actually grew her no-dig gardens on old beds and tables because when she began to produce clean fresh organic food for herself, she was too ill to bend down. Raising the beds is wonderful for the elderly or anyone in a wheelchair.

Setting Up the Raised Bed

Depending on the height of the raised bed, you need to think about how to fill the bed area without unnecessarily using all your good growing resources all the way down to the ground. So here is a step by step guide of what you need to consider and do.

The Design Phases

Step 1   Select the site. This requires a sector analysis and zonal plan so the garden is positioned where it can get water and where it will be used. These are the most important amongst a number of considerations.

Step 2   Decide on the height of garden needed for the age group using it and then measure the arm's reach of the young gardeners. This length will determine the width or the diameter of your garden. If the bed is raised only 20 - 30cm then small foot holds can be placed within the garden for the smaller children to extend their reach.

Any material available is a good place to start, but always check that the material is food grade safe. Treated logs are not a good choice and tyres are known to leach chemicals, so stay away from them. There is a food grade black plastic liner that could be used but choosing natural materials or things created to hold food or water is a better solution.

Old water tanks have been cut down to form 'tank beds' or 'earthrings' and have been so effective, they are now made commercially for this purpose. If using an old tank, ensure the top edge is protected by covering with a hose sliced on one side or buy and fix the black protective strips made for the purpose. You can order an earthring with the edges 'rolled' from a corrugated iron tank manufacturer. The rings need no bottom but if an old tank has one just ensure there is adequate drainage and passage for worms.

If the recycled tank has a diameter wider than the average arm's reach of the children, then sink an old wash tub in the centre that can hold water plants. These require less maintenance so require less reaching. Or place some artwork in the centre as long as it doesn't create too much shade to the shade-aspect side of the garden.

Untreated sleepers are another alternative and of course rocks can be used, but schools need to decide on the appropriate size for safety. Some schools have used hand sized rocks with no problem, while others will find that these may be a temptation, even if only in the early days of the garden, before they are obscured by groundcovers. Any stacked rocks should always be cemented as they can be dislodged through weeding or digging and roll onto little fingers or feet.

Water is the limiting factor to a raised bed, so if you don't have the ability to get water to the garden then perhaps a sunken garden is the better choice. Climatic constraints will influence the garden design, so a hot exposed site will suit a rock and cement raised bed better than the metal earthring.

Once the placement, size and material decisions have been made, then the next consideration is how to build the garden for longevity.

The Construction Phases

Step 3   Rust is the main concern with the earthrings and I always set these onto a gravel base and fill the bottom with gravel for about 4cm inside which ensures good drainage. If you have a sunny position on a cemented area, ensure the metal and cement are not in direct contact as a reaction between the minerals in the cement and the metal of the tank will cause corrosion. Put the ring up on clay pavers and fill the bottom with larger gravel that will not come out of the gap between the cement and the ring. Then fill with a few centimetres of the smaller gravel for drainage.

For building in any material, drainage is important. Growing in a sealed vessel can lead to sour (anaerobic) soil and conditions that are not conducive to the soil biota and worms which are the basic essentials for a healthy productive garden. So leave gaps in log construction and drainage holes in brick or stone construction.

Step 4   Above the drainage layer you can put a filtering membrane such as weed mat or the fabric used to stop siltation on construction sites. This will keep the drainage pathways from silting up and your soil sweet.

If you want to entice earth worms up into your garden then you may need to use some areas of natural materials like cotton or linen so the worms can make their way through this barrier.

Step 5   Depending on the depth of your garden container, you need to add materials to fill and/ or to plant into. For filling, you can add any subsoil, rocks or logs. My choice is old acacia trunks and branches as they are abundant here, they contain nitrogen, will break down slowly as new soil forms on the top of your garden and they have no nasty chemical residue nor are they allopathic in nature so that they do not give out chemicals to retard growth of anything but their own kind. Your 'filler' will take up space between the drainage layer and the growing medium.

Step 6   This is where you need to create your growing layer. The instructions for the layers of the no-dig garden may be applied in this situation. If you want to get a head start, you could add a deep layer of growing medium here. This would be similar to the planting mix for your no-dig garden (above) but used as a layer of about 10 -12 centimetres. Because the garden is off the ground, you do need to ensure there is plenty of nutrition and slow release minerals available for the early years. This can be added through crushed rock, watering in clay colloids (by having lumps of clay in a watering can), adding good composted humus, or by applying a seaweed preparation. Watering in molasses will also stimulate the growth of soil biota that are otherwise well below ground level or have been disturbed and killed by moving the soil and humus into the raised bed. It is also a good idea to introduce worms to the top. (This is explained in the compost or worm pipe step following.) If you have anyone in your community that can brew an aerobic compost tea, this is the time to get their help. But ensure that anyone in the vicinity is wearing a mask when the tea is applied as a fine spray. If it is flicked on with a brush as biodynamic preparations often are, then there is not the same level of concern. Of course biodynamic preparations at this stage will have an important positive effect on the life in your soil and the resulting abundance of the garden bed.

Bringing in the Workers

Step 7   As well as the microscopic soil biota (micro-fauna) the macro-fauna will ensure a healthy and productive garden. Worms can be introduced in the worm castings of your growing mixture or you can introduce them into composting towers and attract them up from the ground.

There are many good books on worms and worm farming and there will be a worm farmer close to the school who will come and give talks to the staff, parents and children. Kids just love worms and they hold a fascination for even those who find them repulsive.

My general but limited understanding is that there are two basic types of worms – the compost worms and earthworms. Compost worms live in the top layer and eat anything that was once alive. They break down this organic matter and make it available to plants and the earthworms that live deeper in the soil. Earthworms will come long distances to find food. The worms that come to feed and work in your garden from the surrounding earth are known as the 'ambient' worms. You don't add these to your garden, although they often come in good potting mixes. Rather you create the conditions for them and they come from miles around. They thrive in a raised garden and can get back out if conditions in the garden are not conducive. This is ideal for gardens that may be shut down, or may go without water for long periods.

Don't be afraid to admit you don't know everything. If you wait until you know everything you won't ever start. Learning about the garden, the creatures and natural systems is a learning journey; an adventure. You just have to get going and learn as you go. In this way the teacher is the facilitator and you are teaching far more than how to grow a garden. You will be teaching children how to learn and to learn for a lifetime. In fact, it is a useful strategy to play down your own skills and knowledge and to allow the children to find the answers for themselves through trial and error, asking people who are skilled, researching using the library or books from friends and family.

Building the Worm Tower

These towers are simply pipes in the ground. They go from ground level or the base of the raised bed, to about 30cm above the top of the growing medium.

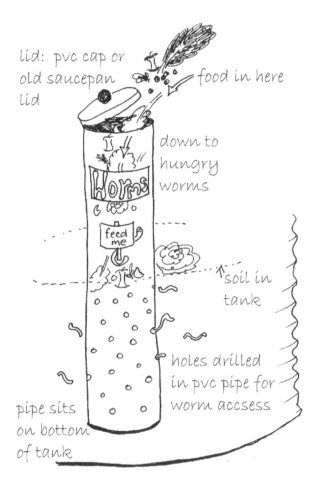

lid: pvc cap or old saucepan lid

food in here

down to hungry worms

worms

feed me

soil in tank

holes drilled in pvc pipe for worm accsess

pipe sits on bottom of tank

Six inch PVC pipes with many holes drilled randomly below the surface of the soil are typically used, but variations occur and still work, depending on the materials available. If concerns are raised about using PVC then clay pipes can be used, however they should sit just above original ground level while still reaching to the 30cm above the top of the growing medium.

A cap or cover of some sort is needed so that the pipe does not become saturated and drown the worms. Compostable materials such as fresh food scraps, light pruning materials or spent plants are put into the pipe along with some dry hay and the compost worms.

The worms eat the dead matter and the ambient worms take the material throughout the garden.

Trials have shown that a garden with a worm tower needs less water than one without a tower. This is probably because food scraps and prunings are 80% or more water and because a soil with worm castings retains water better than a soil with no castings. The towers also make it simple to keep a garden tidy and they clearly demonstrate a closed loop system.

The Planting Phase

Step 8   The planting strategy will depend on the rotation plan and the companion planting decisions as well as the aspect of the garden and the seasonal changes. Children can research and plan the plantings using simple local planting guides or the information from local gardeners. Reading seed packages or the information with seedlings can also be a guide. Never underestimate the value of trial and error and allow children to make mistakes, or to take a chance and then good discussion, research and writing can come out of the consequences (positive and negative).

Planting records kept in the library will help with garden planning and in the understanding of the usefulness of good documentation and the value of learning from previous experience or the experience of others.

If you choose the thick growing layer you are able to grow from seed in your garden from the very first planting, but if you choose the no-dig garden method you will need to start with seedlings till the materials break down, (as per the No-Dig Garden instructions).

The Harvest

Step 9   A group may choose to harvest a bit at a time (as in a 'quick pick' garden), or they may plan for a single harvest.

The single harvest allows for the class to get in and out in a determined period. Following the harvest, the garden may be put to a cover crop, put to rest with compost and hay, or turned over by chickens.

Bring in the Chooks

Using animals in the system is a good way to expand the systems thinking and the idea that humans do not need to do all the work. By adding new elements to the garden, such as chickens, you can reduce the work, reduce the waste and obtain a larger range of products from the garden.

Many schools have chickens which are housed in a strongly protected chicken house and run. These chickens may be brought out into the garden in small cages (known in permaculture as 'chicken tractors') to work in the gardens during the school day. There aren't many more comforting sounds than that of the chickens clucking away in a garden outside the classroom and children will work quietly just to hear them.

If brought out daily to work a section of garden, chickens are very useful in cleaning up the residual growth after a harvest, eating insects, larvae and eggs, scratching in humus and adding manure to the soil. They provide these gardening services as well as giving eggs, feathers, young chickens and (rarely in schoolyards as it can be traumatic for some children) meat. Usually if there is a death of a chicken through old age or misadventure, the beloved chicken is given a burial and the passing is used to illustrate the natural cycle of life by planting a shrub or tree.

Preparing for the Next Planting

Step 10   Once the harvest is complete and the chickens, or the children, have removed and composted the residual plant matter and any weeds, then it is time to ensure there are enough nutrients for the next planting. Some crops are 'hungrier' than others and things like corn will take a lot of nutrient from the soil that must be replaced or put into the garden before replanting.

This understanding of what is lost to a garden when product is taken away and consumed elsewhere is a key element for understanding sustainability issues in all contexts. When nutrient is taken from the garden in the form of fruit or vegetables, then this nutrient must be returned in some form if the garden is to produce as well in the future.

One strategy is to follow one crop with another that takes out different nutrients and/ or adds the nutrients lost to the previous harvest. This is the age-old crop rotation method. Demonstrating the need to plan in this way is an essential learning for children not only to understand the concept of real, practical sustainability but also to gain understanding of nutritional issues when selecting the foods to eat for good health. The concept of different plants accumulating different nutrients forms the basic understanding of a balanced diet. Children need to know the plant sources of iron, potassium, magnesium etc and how to grow or select plants that will deliver optimum nutrition through diversity.

Lessons in recycling through composting, worm farms or chicken systems will teach children how to 'close the loop' so that nutrient is cycled and not allowed to become waste or pollution and run the system down. If your school garden is less vigourous and suffers increased insect attacks in subsequent seasons, then it is almost certain that the garden is loosing nutrient. To trouble shoot this situation you could call in a successful local gardener or shut the garden down as for Step 9 in the 'No-Dig Garden' instructions, and wait for the nutrient levels to increase.

Resting a garden is another old strategy for maintaining nutrient levels which works well in temperate climates where 'fallow' has been used since early agricultural times. Do ensure that the garden does not suffer from 'long fallow' which is the situation when soil biota dies because of the lack of plant cover or organic matter and exposure over an extended period.

In tropical and sub-tropical areas fallow is not an option, as the warm rains will leach nutrients below the roots of most garden vegetables and can be recovered only by comfrey and daikon radish which send roots down 10 - 12 metres. Always ensure there is a cover crop or heavy mulch on gardens in these climates.

If you can keep good rotational planting records, add compost, rest gardens, utilise cover crops and green manures then your school raised-gardens should increase in productivity as the years go by.

Your garden should grow soil every year. In the event of a disaster, just add nutrient and start again. This in itself is a wonderful education for children in gardening and as a lesson to be applied in other aspects of their lives.

The Sunken Garden

This is the reverse of the raised bed and good for hot, dry areas where evaporation may be greater than precipitation. The benefits are:

☞ It can be productive even in areas where there is very little rainfall and where otherwise there would be no school garden

☞ condensation and evaporation are utilised

☞ It demonstrates the principle of edge effect by increasing the growing space and increasing the number of aspects in the one area

☞ water catchment and movement is highly visible in this garden design

☞ It clearly demonstrates full utilization of all water on the site and the moderation of potential flooding

☞ If the garden boundary is large enough, many children can look into the garden and watch demonstrations at the one time

☞ these gardens may be placed in series so that the overflow from one becomes the inflow of the next

Adapted from *Rainwater Harvesting* by Brad Lancaster

Step 1   Find a water catchment that is not yet utilised. This may be a car park, flat cemented area, roof water from a down pipe going directly to storm water or the overflow from a tank, or off a road or pathway gutter. Then work out how this water can be diverted or channeled to an area for a sunken garden.

Step 2   Design the dished out area so the inflow is higher than the outflow and that the outflow can take the overflow water away without damming up and drowning the plants. The outflow may go to a second, or even a series of sunken gardens, before reaching the planned exit point. This point could be the place the water would have ended up before the interventions, or the design may move the water flow away from an exit point that was a problem prior to the intervention. If the water source may have chemical contamination, as in run off from roads or car parks, put the water to a reed bed first and filter out the contaminants.

Step 3   Design the base of the garden so that the sunken dish is lined with a gravel base covered by a siltation barrier fabric. This gravel allows for water to sit in the bottom of the garden for days without waterlogging the garden and allows the plants to draw water up when needed. The top of the gravel needs to be only about 10cm below the outflow level and this 10cm should be the depth of your planting medium layer. In heavy rain events you may lose soil into the overflow but it is easily collected and returned. Your planting strategy and mulching regime will play a large role in keeping the soil in place in a heavy downpour.

Step 4   Select the species for the sunken garden so that those requiring more water are planted further down into the base of the dish, with the dry tolerant species at the rim. Pathways in the garden are best as close to contour as possible because those going straight down, will increase the speed and carrying capacity of the water flow. If you have a series of sunken gardens, then your planting options are greatly increased. Each successive garden will have a decreased risk of flooding and so can have decreased amounts of gravel in the bottom and increased amounts of top soil.

Step 5   Build the garden by excavating the dish/ dishes and the appropriate inflow/ outflow links. These can be quite long (as in diversion drains) but will still flow if they fall slightly over the distance (1:300). Construct the gravel layer with silt membrane and then fill to bottom of the outflow with growing medium (as for the raised garden beds).

Step 6   The mulching layer is very important in dry-land growing, as the water you save is as important as the water you collect. One benefit of the sunken garden is that it shelters the plants and the soil from the drying winds and has some of the garden in shade during the day for most of the year. Don't be afraid to use large rocks at the rim or rocks as mulch in the higher parts of the dish, as the cooler rock surfaces will condense water out of the warmer night air. This water will run down and under the rocks where it can move slowly through the soil keeping it hydrated. The rocks then shelter the soil and create a thermal mass that can moderate fluctuations in temperature. Hay or straw is useful as a 'nutrifying' mulch and when choosing the rich lucerne hay, ensure you cover it with the cheaper straw so that it will not loose its nitrogen to the air. Also consider growing a living mulch or stacking the garden so there is no exposed soil at all. These strategies will ensure reduced evaporation as will the planting of deciduous trees or small leafed legumes to shade the garden in summer.

These sunken gardens can be highly productive in otherwise impossible places to garden and they extend still further, the visible applications of permaculture principles to create wonderful models of systems thinking.

The Keyhole Garden

The benefits of this configuration are:

- It increases the edge effect in the garden
- there is maximum access to all parts of the garden
- the scale can be set for any aged gardener and is calculated on arm reach
- Insect pests are not able to munch their way down straight rows as keyhole gardens allow for bends, twists and curves
- they take advantage of all growing space
- demonstrates the principle of working with nature not against it
- demonstrates the application of pattern for function
- more children can work in the same space than in gardens with straight edges

The name comes from the shape of the garden, which is designed to maximize edge and allow for the best access to the garden.

This designed component is an excellent demonstration of how permaculture uses pattern understanding to advantage and is well described in *'Permaculture, A Designer's Manual'* by Bill Mollison, 1988 page 375.

The garden shape may be a single circle with an access 'keyhole' or it may be a straight or curved edged garden with a series of keyhole accesses. It may be constructed at ground level or it may be a raised bed.

If constructed at ground level the keyholes may be part of a circular mandala garden described later.

Keyhole gardens are an excellent way of demonstrating how patterns in nature can be mimicked to perform the desired function in a designed system such as a garden.

As only the boundary configuration is different in these gardens, the techniques for the No-Dig Garden or the Raised Bed Gardens can be used to build one or a series of keyhole beds.

The Mandala Garden

This has become almost synonymous with the no-dig garden and once again describes the configuration of the boundary and pathways. It was first described by Bill Mollison in his '*Permaculture: A Designer's Manual*', page 269 as the Gangamma's Mandala and well drawn on page 274 of that text.

The word 'mandala' is from the Sanskrit and describes a circle that considers the boundary and the centre at the same time. Mandalas have a spiritual significance and are represented in all the religions of the world. This basic shape and the infinite designs that are possible within it, makes a profound link with those working with universal energies in a garden. The use of this and other universal designs allows permaculture to cross all religious and cultural boundaries. These links make the garden a valuable learning tool for the study of other cultures.

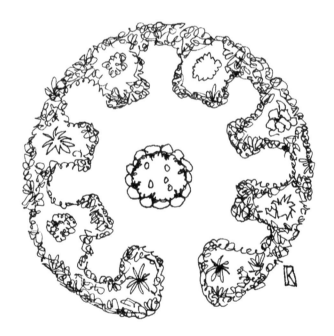

The mandala can be a no-dig garden or a raised bed. It may have a tree or pond in the centre, or some other feature. Paths may cross or circle the garden with keyholes. So the potential for variations of the mandala garden are the same as the variations for mandala designs in art or religion.

Banana Circles

These are a variation of the Gangamma's Mandala, described in *'Permaculture: A Designer's Manual'*, page 275 and is another example of:

- working with natural patterns
- increasing edge
- using all resources available
- producing no waste
- modifying incoming energies
- slowing, filtering and directing water through a site
- using a boggy site for good food production

These circles could be useful in your school if;

- there is a damp area you wish to dry out and utilise
- you have access to storm water that can be diverted and used to produce food
- there is only a small area for food production
- larger compostable materials such as small branches and prunings need to be disposed of and used on the site
- there is a need to filter or slow water
- banana leaves are needed for food preparation and presentation
- one of your garden areas requires shade

All bananas will grow to form a circle, but this is not what we want in a designed system as this growth pattern increases competition for the needed resources.

The banana circle is a pit, 60 to 80cm below ground level at the centre with the dug out materials forming a circular rim mound or bund around it. The circle is typically two metres across but may be a little smaller. Five or seven bananas are spaced evenly on the bund. This configuration allows all the plants access to light and the water that will collect in the pit from the uphill inlet you create. Into this pit is thrown any weeds or prunings as well as the chopped up stems of mother banana plants once they have produced their fruit and the new sucker. As this material breaks down, it forms the nutrient for the producing bananas. The sugars in the banana trimmings stimulate the life in the soil and the decomposition process speeds up.

These circles can be filled to nearly one and a half metres above the ground level with green wastes and they will continually break down so that more may be added. The nutrient from the humus produced, goes to the bananas but is also taken by worms and other soil biota into the wider garden. In this way, a banana circle demonstrates a closed loop system, keeps the garden tidy, produces food and takes up excess water.

As for the sunken garden, these pits with bunds can be arranged in sequence so the outlet of one is the inlet of the next. Water filtration increases with each overflow so the first pits can be considered simply as water filters rather than food producers if the water is from a suspicious source.

Other plants can be substituted for the bananas and this may be needed in areas where government regulations disallow bananas on school grounds. You do need to check with your education department for a list of prohibited species before planning your garden. Giant papyrus makes an excellent filter at either the intake or the expelling points in your designed system. Some people have used paw-paw in circles and Bill Mollison has designed coconut palm circles in the Pacific Islands with great results. The beauty of these strategies is that there are infinite variations depending on the site and the needs.

Maintaining the banana circle is easy as there is good access to each plant, the trash can be cut and thrown directly into the pit. You simply need to decide which way to 'walk' the bananas. As a mother banana is taken down then the daughter, selected as the successor, grows on and any suckers not in the direction of 'travel' are removed and fed to the pit. The surviving preferred sucker is the grand-daughter and will take over when the mother is cut down. In this way, there will only ever be the 5 or 7 plants and their immediate, single successors on the bund.

If you wish to plant water loving species in the pit then this is also an option. Extended edges, aspect options and access to water allows for a diversity of plant species. Dry sun-loving plants would be positioned on the top of the inside and/ or outside of the bund facing north, while sun loving species requiring more water would be below them down into the pit. Shade tolerant species would be placed on the southern side and so forth.

The only concern with these pits, especially in the warmer regions, is the potential for mosquitoes to breed. So it is important that if you need the circle for compost, that it is kept well filled and if it is used for plantings, that those plants are dense and thirsty enough to take up water in order to restrict mosquito breeding.

In some cases it may simply be a matter of increasing the drainage of the pit in mosquito season. This can be done by sandbagging in the cool and/ or dry and removing the barrier in the warm and/ or wet, or by filling the food production pit in mosquito season with green waste.

The banana circle strategy is a clever one and well worth thinking about as a strategy in your school garden. Careful design can make it an excellent design component in your system.

The Herb Spiral

This has similar benefits to the banana circle and is more or less its reverse. The spiral is designed to keep the water intolerant herbs high and dry while providing a variety of aspects.

The benefits of this garden configuration are that:

- many herbs can be grown in the same place as many sun aspects and water access are provided in the one area
- growing space can be doubled by building a mound
- maintenance and harvesting are easy because of the increased edge and circular pathway access
- it requires only two square metres of space and can be directly outside the classroom or kitchen
- the herbs can be used in sensory activities and it may form part of a sensory garden for children with special needs
- the medicinal and cultural significance of the many herbs may form part of science or cultural studies
- the spiral formation of the pathway can be explored in mathematics through the Fibonacci Series, in art lessons or studies of natural demonstrations of the spiral in animal and plant life

Building the Herb Spiral

Step 1   Locate the site and cover with thick newspaper, just as for the no-dig garden and ensure the paper will be under the path as well.

If you wish to add more diversity to the garden, locate the best place for the water to drain and dig a small pond. This is not essential and will depend on the space available and the safety policy of the school. If you do choose to have a pond to take up any nutrient from the mound, create added habitat and provide a more diverse variety of growing niches, then make sure it is deep enough to support small native fish that will eat any mosquito larvae.

Step 2   Build the base of the spiral as a circle with large rocks. You can put a layer of gravel in this circle if your soil is clayey or not free draining. Ring the garden with a substantial path that will prevent grasses or weeds from sending runners into the spiral mound.

Step 3   Locate a source of soil or make a mixture similar to the planting mix for the no-dig garden. Remember that a rich healthy soil will produce herbs of good fragrance and flavour. Then deliver soil (about 1 - 1.5 cubic metres) onto the circular base and place rocks in a winding pattern up the mound.

Step 4   Select the herbs for the spiral and place them in the positions most apt for their needs. Do not plant any of the mint family in a small spiral as it will take over the whole thing. Mint is vigourous and tolerant of many growing conditions. If you do put basil or rosemary in the spiral, do keep it trimmed into a compact plant as both of these tend to get very big.

Step 5   Mulch the whole lot so that it retains moisture. I find that chopping the mulch hay into smaller bits allows the rocks to show as a hard feature of the garden.

Step 6   To keep the herb spiral looking good and producing well, keep the plants well pruned and replace the annuals. Collect the seeds and propagate in other seed-raising beds or in pots. This feature is designed to have a variety of herbs in the one place, so if your students want to grow 'commercial' quantities for sale in markets or to supply local restaurants, then large raised beds for the dry tolerant and another bed for those that like a bit of water is a better strategy.

The thing with herbs is that they are so easy to grow if placed in the right spot. You may have rosemary borders along paths and basil can be a lovely screen in other parts of the school garden. Ginger will grow well in damp and shady places and lemongrass makes a wonderful garden border. So as well as the herb spiral, you can plan to have herbs and spices throughout the school grounds.

Pathways

Pathways can be more than just access for people and a wheel-barrow; they can be areas of water storage, catchments and drainage as well as providing thermal mass and reflective surfaces. Always make the path wider than the width of a wheelbarrow, as plants will grow over the path edges and reduce the width and access.

Never discount an area in the school grounds as a potential garden because of it being too wet or too dry. The pathway design can help overcome some site limitations. The technical discussion of this is really beyond the scope of this book, but it is important that the potential uses of paths and their functions in a garden are known so that experienced garden designers, who understand the concept of multi-functions, can be involved in the design from the beginning.

There are several choices for pathway materials, but any selection must be influenced by the safety considerations for the children who will use it, along with the possible need for wheelchair access and the maintenance and cost issues.

Many schools start with a newspaper barrier or weed mat, with crusher dust on top as a cost effective solution. When the garden use is increased and assured, then longer term surfacing can be used. There are all sorts of recycled products that may be appropriate such as crushed roof tiles and cement.

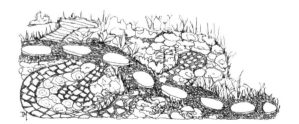

Deciding on the materials for the pathways can be a class activity;

- take in cost issues and budgets, and energy considerations in the production and transport of the materials
- consider the reflective properties of the materials and their effect on surrounding buildings and plants, the need for drainage, weed control issues as well as the aesthetics of the garden
- be very careful with your path materials when working on a slope
- never use cardboard under mulch on a slope as it becomes very slippery when wet

Trellises

The growing area of your garden is significantly increased by using trellises to support climbing plants. These trellises may form all or part of the garden boundary or may be structures over pathways for areas of shade. Specific planting areas may have trellises over them in the form of tepees, or simple lattices constructed from bamboo or string. Trellises may be placed beside a wall; either right against the wall or a metre or two away to provide shade to the wall. Watching plants twine their way up a structure holds endless fascination for children. The way the plant seeks the light and 'feels' its way onto a support and the tendrils it sends out to make a secure attachment, is part of the magic of a garden. There is such excitement when this activity of the plant is then revealed in mathematical terms.

A special form of trellising is the espalier method of tying and training the branches of a fruiting tree to strung wire on a fence or up against a wall. This is an age-old practice and used when space is a constraint. All trellising methods can be related to cultural studies, from the grapes in a vineyard to the citrus espaliered against a stonewall. Plants can also support other plants and when put together in this way the combination is called a 'guild'.

The most famous guild would have to be the Three Sisters of Mexico (beans, corn and squash). The corn supports the growing bean vines, which in return make sure the corn stalk is strong.

The bean provides nitrogen to the squash and the corn, while the squash shades the ground, retains water and controls weeds. Cultural studies can include the Mexican people, their history, art, homes and food. A class may decide to grow corn for tortilla and grow the fillings as well. Learning the origins of fruits and vegetables can give children an insight into the diversity and the trade of the world as well as gaining an understanding of the origin of species and how they have been selected to provide the foods we have today. Learning the endless possibilities for creating guilds allows children the ability to design and grow highly productive gardens as well as having a clear understanding of the win/win situation as opposed to a parasitic relationship.

Getting Enough Water to Your Garden

The different garden designs already described will help with the water needs of your garden, but there are other helpful ways to deliver water to a garden you may wish to explore.

Most often school gardens are allocated to areas that have no other use at the time and so the luxury of using the best place for a garden is rarely an option. But you can use water from the many roofs for the growing spaces.

Utilising Roof Water

Schools have abundant hard surfaces to catch water and most often this precious water is moved off site as quickly as possible through storm water pipes.

Depending on where the school is in relation to industries and air borne pollution, roof water can be a very clean source of water. Drinking-water tanks require a first flush system and some filtering, but the garden-water tank can fill from the roof gutters and then the overflow can go back to the storm water drain. All you need to do is put some storage between the catchment area and the overflow. This can be a very straightforward procedure especially if the roof is high on the site. This allows for the water to fall into the tank and still have enough elevation to be gravity fed to many areas of the school grounds.

If the tank is low in relation to gardens then a small demand-feed pump can be used to move the water and even supply enough pressure for hoses and sprinkler systems.

Children should be able to see where their water comes from, know the capacity of the tank and the catchment area of the roof. They should be aware of the rain events that deliver the water and the usage demands of the garden. As water is the limiting factor to the production of the garden, these links should be made early and reinforced throughout their school years. The concept of water saving (techniques, behaviours and devices) should be part of the garden and the essential resources' studies at all levels.

Clean water for emergency situations is another area that can be addressed in the school grounds. Local indigenous people or those who spend long periods away from tap and bottled water can show the children how to get enough water to keep themselves alive if they become lost or stranded.

Lessons about catching, storing and using water can be part of a safety program, water–wise initiative, cultural studies, mathematics project, auditing process and it may cover several genres of writing or any of the creative arts.

Apart from clean air, that we need every minute, water is something we need daily and we perish if without it for only 3-4 days (and a child perhaps even less than that). For such a basic necessity of life, it is imperative that the school shows its students much more than how to merely turn on a tap and use the stuff.

Fresh water is now one of the most valuable yet limited resources on Earth and will continue to be essential to all living things even as it becomes increasingly scarce.

There is a lot to think about when planning the school grounds. Hopefully the practical advice in this chapter will allow you to create very successful gardens that can provide abundant opportunities for learning across all learning areas, using all the learning styles and increasing the sensory experiences of the children.

Temperate Climates: Experiences from Britain

by Lusi Alderslowe, Cathy Fowler, Steve Smith
edited by Joe Atkinson, illustrations by Jane Bottomley

The average European child spends 90% of their life inside.[1] This can lead to a range of health problems related to poor indoor air quality, lack of exercise and so on. In his book Last Child in the Woods, American writer Richard Louv coined the term 'Nature Deficit Disorder' to describe a range of children's behavioural problems arising from low levels of nature connection.

Conversely, being outside can reduce stress; increase physical activity (helping to reduce obesity); increase one's sense of well-being; increase understanding of nature; improve attention, concentration and confidence to aid academic learning;[2]

"When planned and implemented well, learning outside the classroom contributed significantly to raising standards and improving pupils' personal, social and emotional development."[3]

So why don't we let our children out? In rich countries there's a rising fear of crime and more cars on the roads, which leads to a perception that it is not safe for children to walk or play outside. Consequently, more children get driven to school and after-school groups, exacerbating the problem. There are also more screen-based leisure activities so children tend to watch TV, play video games etc. Finally, access to green space can be difficult, particularly in densely populated urban areas. And that's before we look out of the window to see that it's cold, wet and windy outside!

The good news is that many schools are coming round to the benefits of using the outdoors as an extension of the classroom. Some schools employ sustainability workers to develop and maintain school grounds, support teaching staff to work outdoors, run outdoor sessions, and work on sustainability issues. The rest of this chapter is drawn from the experience of such workers, all of whom have a permaculture background.

Possible Obstacles and How to Overcome Them

1. Perceptions about the weather

Other staff or parents may think that it's too cold or too wet, putting children off before they start.

Solution: wrap up!

Children are happy in all weathers as long as they are adequately dressed. It's best if schools can buy in some waterproof trousers, jackets and Wellington boots for children to wear (and get dirty) when going out. Additionally, schools are often over-heated making it feel much colder when they go out. This is a good opportunity to link to the eco-school curriculum[4] and turn the heating down to 18°C.

2. The Actual Weather

It is sometimes genuinely difficult or dangerous to work in very heavy rain or high winds, or if water-logging or severe frosts make soil unworkable.

Solution: protected cropping

It may be worth having a polytunnel so children can work undercover. A greenhouse and potting shed may also be useful for seed planting etc. Think carefully about cost/benefit: and placement of such structures: they can be vulnerable to severe winds and vandalism.

3. School holidays

Often we get our gardens growing and looking fantastic in April and May, and then after the 6 week summer holiday, the veg patch is total chaos and none of the plants we put there are visible. In addition to the summer holidays, Easter and Spring half-term holidays can be hot and dry when seedlings are most vulnerable.

1   http://europa.eu/rapid/press-release_IP-03-1278_en.htm
2   Sowing the seeds: Reconnecting London's Children with Nature
3   Learning Outside the Classroom. How far should you go? OFSTED
4   http://www.eco-schools.org

Solution: involve the community; select appropriate plants and varieties

Invite parents, grandparents and children to tend plants in the holidays (put the growing area in an accessible location) and create a watering regime, especially for a polytunnel/greenhouse. Plant densely and mulch between plants to reduce watering requirements and suppress 'weeds'.

Select varieties of fruit that will be ready after the summer holidays, such as autumn-fruiting raspberries, blackcurrants, and most top fruit.

Autumn sown crops such as garlic, onions, peas and broad beans can be ready by the summer holidays and should be less vulnerable over Easter and Spring half-term holidays.

Annual crops with a short season – salad potatoes, salad, radishes etc. – may be ready in time to harvest before the holidays. Experiment with cold frames and hot boxes (using heat from fresh manure) to extend the season and get them started early. Note: classroom windowsills are often too warm, resulting in vulnerable plants at planting out time. Is there somewhere cooler to start off seedlings or to harden them off?

Various perennials are ready before the summer holidays such as lovage, welsh onions, numerous herbs, strawberries and so on. There are also various salad crops that can be harvested in the winter, such as winter purslane, salad burnet or winter lettuce.

4. Children not allowed to eat food they have grown.

School chefs might have concerns about the quality and quantities of produce grown in school grounds. In particular, difficulties may arise if the school has contractors for school meals as there is then less choice over menu.

Solution: involve everyone & promote choice

Talk to the kitchen staff about what could be possible. Find out what they would like to cook with and grow accordingly. Also, it may be possible to organise tasting sessions at breaks for example.

When tasting produce with children whilst gardening, do the tasting at the start of the session when little hands are less likely to be muddy. A word of warning – this can use up the whole session with

eating wild strawberries rather than weeding - but that is a great outcome in itself. Many children are willing to try even obscure vegetables and fruit, but it is important to retain the element of choice.

When choosing fruit to grow, choose varieties that can be eaten straight from the tree rather than those that need a period of storage before the flavour develops: storage space may be an issue and the prized fruit may be forgotten by the time they are ready.

Varieties local to the area may do particularly well as well as providing an element of historical interest.

"As there was not a food-growing culture in our community in Glasgow, there were many misconceptions in schools. Many parents and teachers believed children were not allowed to eat the produce that was grown by the children on school grounds. On a school visit from Prince Charles, this was brought to his attention. He brought the whole event to a standstill with his surprised remarks and 2 weeks later raised it at a major food conference. Now Glasgow is awash with schools confident to engage their pupils in food-growing."

5. Young trees being damaged by grounds maintenance contractors

Despite communicating with the local authority, contractors and education board, messages are often not passed down to the individual who is mowing the grass. Even if he receives the message, he must be able to see the small trees and take extra time and care to mow around them.

Solution: tell EVERYONE and make the trees highly visible

The safest system is to inform everyone in the authorities, the mowers themselves (they often are different people every week), and put up sturdy edging or fencing around young trees with clear signs. Use hazard tape and site pegs to create a visual barrier for newly planted hedges. Ensure that trees have a good sized area around their base that is weeded and mulched: contractors will be less likely to strim up close to the trunk.

6. Local authority bureaucracy

This can slow the processes of gaining permission to use land or making changes to infrastructure. School staff can be dragged to long meetings which can drain enthusiasm and the reduce time available

for session planning. The whole school can become disheartened due to delays.

Solution: sell the benefits; value the marginal

Involve the local community and highlight other successful projects in order to get local press, councillors, education board etc supporting the project.

Often hedges can provide a fantastic resource along existing site boundaries without taking up too much space – they are a great resource as a habitat, linear tree trail or food supply. Check what plans are for future developments and which areas are designated for sports etc.

7. Vandalism

In many places, vandalism can destroy newly created gardens.

Solution: the problem is the solution

Vandalism can be reduced by opening up access to gardens – not fencing them off – and involving the local community in re-building anything which has been vandalised (using inexpensive materials). This turns the problem of vandalism into opportunities to involve local people, build community, provide out-of-hours surveillance, and to create alternative, positive activities for local young people.

Seasonal Curriculum Links

Curriculum connections are covered in depth in Part IV. Here are some curriculum links that are specific to the seasons in cool climates.

Term	Activity	Curriculum link
Autumn	Harvesting, harvest festival, Apple Day	Healthy eating
	Planting – spring bulbs, perennials, green manures, some onions, garlic, salads under cover, broad beans	Healthy eating Science – How plants grow
	Insect hunts, pond dipping	Science
	Tree planting, willow weaving. (while trees are dormant – i.e. when they have no leaves up until March)	Geography – Looking after environment Art
	Feeding birds, making bird feeders	Science – What animals need to survive Design and Technology
Spring	Schools birdwatch	Various. See: www.rspb.org.ul/schoolswatch
	Nest box week	Design and technology, Science – Habitats
	Planting indoors, out if warm microclimate	Science – How plants grow
Summer	Harvesting early sown crops Planting crops to last over summer holidays	

Sources of Support

There are various initiatives and organisations that can support learning in the outdoors. Their websites have various resources both for developing the grounds and for lesson plans. In the UK, they include:

Learning through Landscapes
Council for Learning Outside the Classroom
Garden Organic (HDRA)
Royal Society for the Protection of Birds
Eco schools
Healthy Schools
RHS – Campaign for School Gardening
Woodland Trust – Nature Detectives
Morrisons – Let's Grow

Support is also available through developing a good role for local businesses in the school community. They can provide volunteers, in-kind gifts or even funding towards outdoor developments through their corporate social responsibility (CSR) schemes.

Case Study: Lower Fields Primary School (Ages 3-11)

Lower Fields Primary School is based in the East Bowling area of Bradford and converted from a middle school (ages 9-13) to primary in 2000. The school has 450 children and is less than 3 miles from the city centre, surrounded by industry and major roads. The catchment area includes a number of 'areas of multiple deprivation', so staff face issues that come with poverty alongside those of a busy inner city primary school.

As a former middle school, Lower Fields inherited a generous amount of land sited on a former landfill waste site. Work began on developing the grounds for improved wildlife value while still a middle school. Since becoming a primary, it has further developed the grounds through partnerships with local environmental education charities and businesses.

Outdoor resources include:

◎ Wildlife area with pond, woodland, wildflower meadow and hedgerows.

◎ Horticulture area with orchard and soft fruit, grow beds for every class, polytunnel and compost bins. A water butt is connected to the roof to use for watering the gardens. It has been painted by students to demonstrate the water cycle.

◎ Kinaesthetic Adventure Park where classes can bring their topics to life, through, for example seeing how life was on the battlefields of Scutari, or for a Roman soldier.

◎ Amphitheatre for outdoor events.

◎ Human sundial.

◎ Outdoor classrooms.

◎ Trim trail.

◎ Willow sculptures.

◎ Geology trail.

Staff are encouraged to make as much use of the outdoors as possible and are supported in this by a Sustainability Team consisting of a Sustainability Manager and two part time Sustainable School Development Workers. The role of the Development

Workers includes the maintenance and development of the outdoor resources, responding to consultation with staff about what would be most useful for their lessons. They also prepare and lead sessions, meaning that teaching staff do not have to be experts in order to get their pupils outdoors. Other parts of this role include developing resources to incorporate sustainability into the curriculum and facilitating the eco team.

Regular outdoor activities include bulb planting, minibeast hunts and pond dipping. Year 4 children (age 8-9) make decisions on improving the grounds and then carry out the work suggested as part of Geography. Children are regularly taken outside as part of many lessons including numeracy and literacy, science and art. Each class has at least one week per term in the Kinaesthetic Adventure Park, the hands on approach demonstrating benefits for children of all ages and abilities. Every class has their own grow bed, meaning that each child should have experience of growing and harvesting at least 6 crops over the course of their school life.

Whilst it may appear a luxury to employ extra staff, relationships developed by the Sustainability Manager have long reaching benefits for the school and wider community. A number of local businesses offer support by providing volunteers as part of their corporate social responsibility programs to help in the grounds as well as in the classrooms and for events such as the Christmas Fair. They also provide materials and funds towards initiatives in the school, the total value including volunteer time being over £250,000, making it well worth the investment. Pupils also take part in events in the community, working alongside the business partners. The Sustainability Manager has also delivered training to staff from local schools, resulting in at least two others creating a similar role within their own school.

Other examples of sustainability in action at Lower Fields include:

◎ The school kitchen prepares food from scratch on site rather than importing pre-packed food for meals. They use the local butcher for meat delivery reducing the distance travelled and enabling him to employ more staff. The staff are supportive of the garden and are open to using crops in their dishes.

◎ Developments in the waste collection contract as a result of a request by the eco-team have meant that none of the day to day waste is sent to landfill. This includes the collection of all food waste to be composted, recycling of as much waste as possible and the rest being sent to a combined heat and power plant. Key stage 1 (ages 5-7) fruit and vegetable leftovers are collected by older children and composted on site.

◎ Recent building developments on site have aimed to reduce energy usage whilst improving educational attainment through more sympathetic design of classrooms.

The school believes in embedding Sustainability within the core areas of campus, community and curriculum, as well as in the benefits of using nature as a teacher and the importance of learning outdoors. It is through this vision that they are a hub of the community delivering not only educational achievement but skills to last their pupils through to the next generation.

Case Study: Colne Valley Specialist Arts College (Ages 11-16)

This 1,500 pupil school serves the entire Colne Valley in West Yorkshire's Pennine uplands. It used to have its own farm which provided students with the opportunity to undertake a 'Rural Studies' course, developing skills in farming, vegetable growing and animal husbandry. Perceived not to fit well with the need for more academic outcomes, the farm was shut down and put into deep storage in the late 1990s.

Fast forward 10 years and the Colne Valley, if not quite experiencing a green revolution, is starting to take more notice of the potential of its landscape, farming heritage and the needs of future generations for sustainability skills and attitudes. The launch of a Transition Town, emergence of local ethical businesses and a growing appreciation of the need for community resilience refocused attention on the high school as a vital community resource. Although fond memories of the school's farm provided momentum there was now an opportunity to address pressing issues and connect both internally with the school and curriculum and externally with the wider community.

The first step was to link with enthusiastic school staff to set up an after-school gardening club. This positive engagement quickly led to a more formal taught course aimed at students who were not being engaged by classroom teaching. Modules in 'Growing and Gardening' were delivered, in school time, by a local community food project, 'Edibles'.

The next step introduced an accredited GCSE-level course, 'Growing and Sustainable Living', aimed at students who were keen to learn outdoors but who struggled with more academic, classroom based teaching. It combines practical food growing skills with a broad introduction to sustainability issues such as energy, transport, water/soil/woodland management, permaculture design, green building, ethical enterprise, wildlife and sustainable communities. Students have planted a forest garden, made compost, grown vegetables, visited renewable energy installations, interviewed the local Member of Parliament (in a field), developed a salad-growing business and spent a day analysing soil at the local university.

The next phase will address two specific challenges; how this initiative can benefit and engage the whole school and wider community, and how to break through the commonly-held perception that practical, outdoor learning is of a lower status than indoor teaching. A more academic course called 'Environment and Sustainability' is planned. Aimed at higher achieving students, it will bring sustainability issues firmly into the curriculum and provide the crossover between indoor and outdoor teaching.

Colne Valley Specialist Arts College's journey is still a work in progress. Learning and progress has been fast, intense and exciting. Some key learning to date includes:

Seek the support of and work closely with senior management and the head teacher. Nothing will happen in a school without the support of the management team. A compelling case needs to be made showing the multiple benefits and synergies education for sustainability can provide and how the outdoors can add considerable educational and functional value.

Outsider and insider benefit. New insights, creative ways of working and additional skills and experience can be brought into the learning environment through schools working with sustainability practitioners, community groups, NGOs, local businesses, academics etc. Schools also have a wealth of experienced education professionals who know what they are talking about. Connect, pool resources and learn from each other.

Avoid stigma and ghetto mentality. Elevate the status of outdoor teaching and the learning of practical skills. Make it a whole school initiative and aim to involve all levels of ability and parts of the curriculum. Avoid the 'outdoor classroom' being seen as a place for eco students and non achievers.

Accredit. The status of sustainability education and the links to the rest of the curriculum will be enhanced by running 'proper' accredited courses. It provides a rigour to teaching and shouldn't challenge the commitment to experiential, experimental, outdoor learning.

Look backwards and forwards. Work with the whole school pyramid in your area. Gain support, validation and enthusiasm for your courses from the schools that you receive children from as well as those that students progress on to. Students are more likely to opt for sustainability courses if encouraged at primary levels and they achieve recognition as they move into colleges and university. Apprenticeships also provide an excellent option for student progression.

The future will be in the hands of the next generations. Schools can be key players in providing working examples of sustainability and equipping children with the values and skills to address the challenges we face.

Find out more:
www.cvsac.org.uk
www.edibles.org.uk
www.mastt.org.uk

Garden Use is Garden Maintenance

Maintenance is an essential aspect of the garden design and should not be left as an afterthought. Understanding the needs of the users, their time and energy, in conjunction with working with nature to achieve the most productive garden with the least waste and work, will ensure your school garden will be successful in the long term. Gardens can fail because they become overgrown and look unloved, which makes them appear difficult, daunting and time consuming to manage.

As discussed in previous chapters, the design for maintenance should include both the physical garden space and the invisible systems and networks that support it. The more groups that use the garden, the more chance it has to be well looked after, remaining attractive and appealing to teachers and learners.

If the energy for maintenance is coming solely from within the school itself, then the position of the garden is most important. In this case, the garden must be close to existing learning activity areas. Placing a garden out of sight or a long way from classrooms will ensure it is rarely used, used only by the faithful or will require an extra playground duty to increase its use. (This is enough to turn any teacher sour on the garden idea). So start small and close to rooms where the garden can be monitored by children and staff and used in or out of class time. If that is not practical then consider building an outdoor shelter close to the garden.

The style of garden bed construction will greatly influence the ease or difficulty of maintenance. Raised garden beds are easier to maintain than those on the ground that can easily be overrun by grass.

Consider using untreated sleepers, water tank rounds or interlocking blocks. Raised beds provide better drainage. Paved or cement pathways are also easier to maintain than gravel or grass; but surfacing decisions do depend on many parameters such as funding, water availability, heat and reflection issues, the commitment to long term garden strategies and so on.

School gardens will be as diverse as the schools that build them, but they all will need to be maintained. So here are some generic suggestions for garden use and maintenance that will apply in some part to most school garden situations.

During the School Term

School days ensure you have access to plenty of hands in the garden. How the garden is used will influence its maintenance and upkeep and so let's look first at the ways gardens can be used by different schools with different needs and resources.

Daily activities by one or many classes can be easily rostered and co-ordinated by using a simple task wheel for the daily work. The wheel can be adjusted for the grade level and the planning scheme for garden use adopted by the school.

Special jobs in the garden are easily linked to other areas of the curriculum and can be set at the same petal in all classes/ grades or the jobs can be staggered. This example shows nine different activities, but you can come up with your own choices.

Very often a school will begin with one garden-use plan and it then evolves into another over time. Schools that have had gardens for 30 years or more will refer to the different 'phases' the garden has passed through and they generally see the garden evolving continuously into the future.

The initial usage will always depend on the reason or stimulus for establishment. Then it may morph, perhaps many times, because of the following catalysts of change:

- staff turn over (and especially when it is the principal)
- new need for the space the garden is using
- new land released through loss of demountable classrooms
- new government initiatives (sustainable schools, healthy eating, water wise etc)
- removal of support for garden-based initiatives
- changing curriculum and/ or pedagogical requirements from education departments
- demands from the community to deliver learning outcomes that they identify as important for their children
- societal shifts
- access to clean, fresh food
- water limitations
- teacher training
- combined skills and knowledge

Garden Usage Plans

1. The School and Community Garden Combined

Having a community garden in or attached to the school garden is a good solution. Often communities want to start a garden but don't have access to land in a central position. Schools are central to their community and often have land that can be used for a garden. Sharing the space can be as simple as a roster for use in or out of school hours, or one section can be fenced off for children-only use in school time.

If the interest in a school garden is small then ensure you start small and build on the participation before extending the garden. This partnership can only exist if there is a good relationship between the school and its wider community and does require a special sort of facilitator/ driver.

At any time this garden can be run exclusively by one partner or the other or both and so has a good chance to be successful in the long term. Having the confidence that the garden will continue, gives teachers the security to invest a lot of their planning and programming time into incorporating the garden into the curriculum. Once teachers are sure the garden has a future, they usually get on board and come up with some amazing lessons to engage their students in new and exciting ways. This work in turn secures the maintenance and future of the garden.

2. The Garden as a Base for a Parent as the Visiting Garden Expert.

Many schools have an area devoted to a garden where one or more parents can take a few children at a time to work in the garden. My friend did this for several years. He began as a volunteer, built a very productive and robust garden (that remains today in a 'latent' phase), which was found to be so valuable to children with classroom behavioural problems that he was employed with money from a government initiative targeting discipline problems in schools identified as 'disadvantaged'.

This worked well for a time, with the children he mentored showing little or no behavioural problems when working outside and improved behaviour in the classroom. But it wasn't too long before the other children began to resent the special privileges given to those who appeared to be rewarded for not working well in class. So the garden was then extended to allow groups of children with a teacher to work in the garden alongside the parent helper. That particular school garden has since had alternating periods of latency and activity, as other parents have taken on the role of garden co-ordinator or visiting garden expert.

The visiting expert generally:

- works with small groups
- ensures the maintenance of the garden
- gives suggested activity ideas to interested teachers
- and supports teachers in having a class working in the garden

Whether the teacher is in the classroom with some children while the parent/ expert is in the garden with others, or both teacher and parent are in the garden with the whole class, will depend on the specific situation at the school and the skill base or qualifications of the parent.

This is a garden that can be flashed up into use very easily or shut down just as easily because of the initial excellent design. Interested teachers and keen parents have sound infrastructure understanding so that the garden can morph at any time in response to any of the 'catalysts of change' listed above.

The maintenance for this garden would come from the parent and directed children as part of the gardening experience. But it is still a garden just about gardening, which is on the outer edge of the learning activities of the school and is really an extension and not part of the day to day learning activity in the classrooms.

3. The Garden for a Garden Club

This is when a garden is used at special times of the week as a chosen alternative to a variety of other activities such as sports, arts, crafts, gymnastics, creative writing and so on. This one off weekly work in the garden is often supplemented by lunch-time participation supervised by a supportive or duty teacher. (If the garden is out of sight of the teacher on playground duty, this added gardening time creates the need for another duty and can make the garden unpopular with the staff on the roster.) This system has worked in some schools for years, and although very valuable, never really demonstrates the full learning potential of the garden when linked to the curriculum.

The Garden Club can be a good solution which allows a garden to be in a holding phase and ensures the infrastructure remains in tact until the full learning potential can be realised.

4. The Garden Providing Produce to a School Kitchen

1. This is an exciting initiative for schools, driven in recent times by Stephanie Alexander as a response to the poor eating choices of young Australians. The Kitchen Garden Foundation was set up to "develop life-long healthier and happier eating habits in a new generation of Australians by engaging them in growing, harvesting, preparing and sharing healthy food at primary school." (The Kitchen Garden Story 06/07 Annual Report).

The foundation has been successful in establishing school gardens and kitchens in many primary schools across initially in Victoria where the need for them was demonstrated by a lack of knowledge of the natural world and of where food comes from. It now looks as if the impact of this most valuable and growing educational movement will be felt in other states as well.

As children and society itself, becomes further removed from the sources of the food that nourishes and sustains them, parents and teachers try to reconnect children with their simple basic needs and how they can be obtained for the best quality life in the long term.

Even if a school cannot afford full demonstration kitchens and dining areas, the children can connect with their food source by growing herbs and vegetables in the school grounds which can be grown, distributed and eaten in the following ways:

2. Classes can grow a salad, stir-fry or a pizza in boxes on verandas or in pots in sunny positions. This produce can be used in a lesson that may or may not be related to other areas of the curriculum. Outdoor cooking equipment may be used for the cooking or electric woks may be brought into the classroom.

3. The produce can go into the canteen to be used in the preparation of healthy lunches.

4. The produce may be put on a stall, so mums or dads can pick up fresh vegetables at the school gate when they collect their children.

5. Children can take the skills learned in the school garden, some seeds or cuttings and work with parents or grandparents to grow, prepare and serve fresh, healthy real food at home.

In many schools in poor third world countries, school gardens provide growing children with fresh food for survival. In these places the school garden is essential to give the children the energy to learn, but it is becoming more and more apparent that children in affluent countries are also suffering from a form of malnutrition, by consuming too many empty calories. Without fresh, clean, healthy food children are unable to meet their full potential in learning, growth or in physical activity.

5. The Food Production or Market Garden

As described above, some schools need to provide food for their students and so need to grow quite large quantities and a wide variety of vegetables and fruits. Larger school gardens can supply local markets and restaurants with produce and can be used to teach mathematics as it relates to budgets and marketing. These real economic situations can provide upper grade classes with valuable practical experiences.

How productive and thereby profitable a garden can be, depends on the weed control and planting regime and so this garden is assured of good care during the school term and can be shut down during the breaks. If it is really productive, then it may be carried over the holidays by someone who can make use of the produce.

6. The Garden as a Cultural Garden

This is popular with schools in multicultural communities. Apart from 'welcome' in 26 languages on the office and library doors, there are often very few visual signs that reflect the different cultural backgrounds of the children attending the school. In some cases the community can be quite fragmented, with little cultural crossover which could deepen understanding that goes beyond mere racial tolerance.

School gardens can offer this cultural crossroad by encouraging each community to contribute their heritage food and growing techniques to the school garden. This is sometimes the only opportunity for the grandparents to be involved and recognized for their knowledge and to be honoured for the special cultural history they are able to share with all sectors of the school community. Many of these older people have struggled with English as a second language and/ or have low levels of numeracy (or the vocabulary to explain it). So they are not able to participate in most learning support programs, but in the garden they become marvellous, confident authorities.

Some schools have different areas for the different cultures because the plants require different temperatures and amounts of water. From a design perspective, it is easier to keep the growing areas separate, but then it is necessary to have a central area where all the participants can meet and share garden tips and a cup of tea. This area can also function as an outdoor kitchen with a cob, or other oven, to demonstrate different cooking techniques as well as function as the area where children come to learn from the elders in the garden and to celebrate the harvest and/ or special cultural days.

The maintenance regime of this garden would be similar to having a community garden in the school as well as having the visiting parent expert. So there may be a variety of usage plans running at the same time. The bonus with the Cultural Garden is that it has more opportunities to be linked to what happens in the classroom, especially around cultural studies.

It is often difficult to get a feel for other cultures in a classroom where books, films and visitors are the only window to the world. The real and authentic experience of working with a person from another culture to grow, prepare and eat unusual foods is something meaningful and memorable for children. The many opportunities to see the differences and similarities between the cultures, how they think about things and go about doing things, can lead children to an understanding of the universal needs, hopes and desires of all mankind. Cultural Gardens also provide an opportunity to understand the impact of climate, access to resources, language and traditions on the way people think and feel today.

Because of the possible commitment from the community and the importance of the messages from a Cultural Garden and its significance in the curriculum, this garden has the opportunity to attract funding from government and commitment from the wider and school communities. This means it has a greater chance of good planning, establishment, maintenance and therefore longevity.

A Special Cultural Garden for Australians – The Bush Tucker Garden

Whether there are aboriginal children attending the school or not, the bush tucker garden is an essential garden component in Australian schools. The local bush tucker plants are sure to grow well in your area if given the chance to beat the grass and concrete. The native garden is an opportunity to engage the local indigenous people. This very often will create a connection so that aboriginal art, history, craft and story telling can all be introduced to the children of the school with the garden as the centre.

7. The Garden For a Specialist Teacher

Some schools choose to use a teaching staff member as a Garden Specialist Teacher. They may have some other special training such as physical education, music, library or a second language. They are usually employed to develop and deliver a garden program in conjunction with the class teacher and/ or the Whole School Planning Document. Depending on the school, the specialist may handle all the planning and delivery of lessons in, or about, the garden. Or they may work with teachers to develop units of study that cross many of the areas of the curriculum.

The maintenance of the garden comes as a result of the activities in the garden. Quite often this teacher has a year plan for the garden and has created a roster for classes so that any garden maintenance work is shared across all classes. The garden specialist teacher is a great support to teachers who are learning gardening skills along with the children. This guidance and support allows the classroom teacher to make the all important connections between work in the room and the activities in the garden.

8. The One Class Garden

This can be very simple and effective for a class with an enthusiastic teacher who sees the value for the group in engaging with the outdoors. A teacher may take over a garden close to the room or a problematic area in the school. Once again, the maintenance will come from the activities and if the teacher moves away from the school, then this garden can revert to the care of the grounds-man. I have had this type of garden at different times and have found great benefits in even having window boxes or pots outside the door.

9. The Garden for Whole School Planning

This is a very exciting situation where the value of the school garden has been acknowledged by many or most staff members and they come together to plan a succession of learning experiences around the garden. How they do that is covered in the curriculum chapter.

It is only left to say here, that these gardens have the best chance of use and maintenance as they are valued places of learning.

Classes may book in to the different garden components required by the units of work they are doing. They may share with other classes the running of that space or they may use it exclusively for some weeks or a term. The roster may be co-ordinated by the garden specialist teacher, a parent supporter, an interested teacher or the principal. If there is no special group using an area during the term, it may be shut down using any of the suggestions for holidays that follow. Once teachers understand that the garden can be utilised for learning and isn't going to be a burden, then they are more likely to become involved and support the outdoor learning program.

Holiday Maintenance

In Australia there are 40-42 teaching weeks with 10-12 weeks of holidays each year, and although this varies in different systems, countries and hemispheres, schools everywhere will share the challenges of keeping a garden going for a period in all of the four seasons during school holidays.

Our big challenge in Australia is the six week Christmas holiday in our hot summer. If your school can carry a garden over in that situation, the rest of the shorter breaks in gentler seasons are easy. So let's look at the big one first.

The Long Hot Christmas Holidays (or the Summer Break in Other Countries)

Classes finish in Australian schools around the middle of December and don't begin again until the end of January or early February so one or more of the strategies outlined below may prove useful.

Shutting a Garden Down

This is described in the Permaculture chapter and basically involves one of the following:

1. Plant a cover crop that can be used as composting materials or that will be dug back into the soil. The crop may be any of the beans, cow peas or pigeon pea as nitrogen fixers or sweet potato.

Any garden store will have advice on the best cover crop for your region in summer. Never use anything that could become a weed as a cover crop. Use things like mint and other vigourous plants with tenacious root systems in places where they will not compete with annual or perennial crops.

2. Plant out the garden with hardy flowers like marigolds or daisies and return to a burst of welcoming colour in the new school year.

3. Pile on manures, prunings and spent plants from other gardens and top with very thick hay and turn the garden to a composting worm farm for 6 weeks so that it is rich and ready to go when school resumes. Just because it stays tidy for 6 weeks, don't push your luck and leave it too long after school resumes to rake over and plant out. As the mulch breaks down, any seed arriving there will germinate.

4. Place fitted fabric covers over the garden and tie them down. You could use a very dense shade cloth, weed mat or hessian. These work best on raised beds.

5. Tank gardens or earthrings may have round timber covers with a slightly larger diameter than the tank which can be placed on the rim of the ring to shut the garden down or to add a potting work station in the garden area. (Tack on hose or timber chucks to ensure a seal so the lid won't slide when in use as a work-bench.)

6. These timber circles can be brightly coloured and stored on otherwise plain walls when not needed. Such covered gardens may be filled with manure and mushroom spores so that you can return to a garden full of mushrooms and a unit on fungi. (Make sure that masks are worn when working in this bed or when lifting any of these exclusion lids as there may be mould and fungi underneath that could irritate some children.)

Find Alternate Users of the Garden

1. Strip the plants out, mulch and leave the garden fallow. Then encourage the holiday care group to use the garden over the six weeks as an extension of the program they run.

They may even want to take it over as you leave it. The children that come for the holidays are usually very excited about getting into the garden, planting it up and preparing meals and snacks with the produce. As long as it is clear how you want to find the garden in the new school year, sharing with the holiday program is a very satisfactory solution.

2. Plant a crop that can be harvested by the cleaning and grounds' staff who work in the school during the holidays. I use cucumbers, watermelon and some of the Asian vegetables, but other regions may carry tomatoes and additional species. Even if the cleaners don't harvest the vegetables, the plant material will ensure that few weeds can volunteer into your garden.

3. Neighbours could be asked to keep an eye on the garden and having something to harvest is an added bonus to get them there regularly.

4. Perhaps some keen local gardeners, parents or teachers interested in self-sufficiency, may wish to use the garden to run a series of workshops for local people during those weeks of reduced use by the school children. You just have to make sure that they know when you want to use the garden again and how you want it left.

5. Upper school students or even students from nearby secondary schools may use the garden for a special project over the break. There are safety and access issues around this sort of use and decisions will depend on the circumstances and the policy of the school or the Education Department in your state.

Simply Let the Garden Go

The other option is to let the garden go 'wild' and use the effort to restore it as lessons in garden maintenance. In this way, you will have the chance to show how quickly a well-designed garden can be returned to full production:

- by chopping and dropping the weeds and establishing a no-dig garden on the old bed site, you can be planting within hours

- by bringing in the chooks and putting them to work in a chicken tractor for a week

- by using lots of willing hands just back from holidays, to remove the weeds, turn them into compost and replace that lost nutrient with materials from a mature compost heap

If you can manage the summer holidays, then the others have to be easy.

Autumn Break

The next challenge is the Easter holiday. This is the autumn break for the southern hemisphere. As Easter varies with the moon cycle, it is hard to pin down but is generally somewhere in late March or the early part of April, so in Australia we are looking at two weeks in autumn.

1. Strawberries can go in before the holidays. You could divide the old runners before the break (the runners must be divided and replanted at least every 3rd year or they won't produce) and plant them out that last week of term and water them in well. Make sure that you have all your runners in by Anzac Day at the latest if you expect a good crop.

2. Plant chrysanthemums so they will be ready in May for Mother's Day and let them fill the bed if you can spare the room for that length of time.

3. Use a planting guide to help with planting choices and keep in mind units of study that may be happening early in the next term. For example autumn is a good season for Mediterranean vegetables in most regions, so maybe a pizza garden can be planted up before the holidays.

Winter Break

In Australia these holidays fall some time in June or July depending on the state.

Because of the shorter daylight hours and cooler temperatures, gardens don't tend to get too out of control in this break even if left alone.

1. In the temperate regions this can be a very productive time for winter vegetables. You just need to ensure your gardens are planted densely and mulched (not too heavily if you expect frosts), so you will return to a good crop to harvest.

2. In the tropics and subtropics, this is the best time for you to do well with European vegetables. In summer your gardens will do better with Asian and tropical vegetables, but the cooler drier days allow the opportunity for abundant European vegetables. So make sure they are planted before the holidays and that there is someone who can water twice a week if necessary.

3. Plant a nitrogen fixing crop such as Lucerne or clover and dig in when school resumes.

4. Of course you can shut down the garden or use any strategies suggested for other holidays. The only risk in these holidays is the unseasonal hot days with no rain and dry winds or frost. If this is the case in your school, then your good planning will tell. You will probably have planted good windbreaks for protection, or you will have selected a high corner in the school yard. Stone or brick walls can help with thermal mass in these situations and so make the most of these protected and cosy corners if you do expect frost. Berries and stone fruit and even citrus can benefit from the cooler positions.

Spring Break

This is the September and October break in Australia. Everyone loves to be in the garden in the spring.

1. Workshops will be a viable option at this time to keep the garden going.

2. If not, it is very likely that it will chug along nicely by itself.

3. Letting the nasturtiums, or other hardy flowers of this season, run over the garden is a colourful suggestion for this break. Just ensure they will go away and stay away (in the main) when you want to put the garden back into production.

4. Once again check the local planting guide as well as the units selected for the following term before making the planting or resting plan for the garden.

Garden Security

Some schools may be in locations that make them vulnerable to the attention of idle hands and fear the intrusion of vandals. This whole-community problem is often evidenced in the local school grounds.

This situation should never become an obstacle to establishing a garden. Before considering exclusion fencing, put in a small and well-loved plot. Very often these are left alone while the 'harder' surfaces of the school are still targeted.

More often fences are needed to exclude the bush turkeys or dogs that have a keen eye on the chicken house. Fencing can also be useful growing structures and will define the area.

Although fences are useful, the best security for a garden is the number of people who care for it. A garden has a good chance of escaping the negative attention of vandals if it is well loved and watched by the children, their families and neighbours.

Part III

Outdoor Classrooms

The idea that school grounds can be learning sites is exciting news for children. If we were to give the grounds over to them, the playground would be filled with animals and plants, places to play in the soil, creeks with running water with trees and rocks to climb. It would be a natural wilderness with lookout towers, caves and cubbies, swings and tree houses, forests, fields and more.

Imagine if we created the landscapes that children love so much and developed them in ways that they would become outdoor classrooms; places where children would not only play, but where they would go with their teacher to learn about a topic in science or history, or in any other subject area of the curriculum.

The school garden is a fine example of an outdoor classroom, probably the foremost exemplar, but we need not stop there. We can stretch the concept of outdoor learning to include other designs that will increase the opportunity for teachers to use the outdoors as a teaching resource while addressing at the same time, the children's loss of natural outdoor places for play.

In this section of the book, I look at the outdoor classroom, first as a design concept with its aims, form and functions and then as a structure/ building for the grounds. This is followed by a collection of ideas for outdoor classrooms which are called, Outdoor Learning Adventures.

A Design Concept

The Outdoor Classroom is a design concept for developing school grounds. It is a developmental tool to enhance and value the use of school grounds for learning. It addresses issues associated with teaching and learning practices, play, environmental and structural design and sensitive landscaping for ecological awareness.

It is a plan that dismantles the traditional view that the grounds are for sport and play and the classroom the place for learning. It is a plan for new functions and new forms for school grounds.

The Aims of an Outdoor Classroom Plan is to:

- value the school ground as a proper place for children's development
- use the outdoors for educational purposes
- add resources for learning to the grounds
- Improve the environmental quality of the grounds
- extend the range of play areas
- address children's loss of natural outdoor areas for play
- connect children to the natural world
- offer cross-curricular and non-discipline-specific learning

Outdoor classrooms are designs for schoolground development. The designs will vary in form but they have a common function to:

- be used by teachers as teaching sites
- be play areas
- encourage curiosity
- direct children's own learning
- Increase the opportunity for creativity
- make learning interactive and place-based
- link curriculum to outdoor activities
- Involve multi-age groups for succession purposes
- Interact with the landscape

89

The Form of an Outdoor Classroom

Outdoor classrooms vary in form. Some are natural sites containing plants and landscaping elements such as rocks and water, for example, whereas others are built sites that use a permanent structure as the main feature. Most places will include both natural and built elements in their design.

A design focus of 'less is more' is appropriate, as children like to use their imaginations to complete the picture. Minimisation of the elements in the design will augur well for safety and maintenance of areas.

Constraints and Possibilities

The school ground is an environment that presents both constraints and possibilities for development. School grounds are not uniform in any aspect. The area of land that a school has today for outdoor activity is dependent on many factors; what the initial allocation of land was, where it is sited, the level of growth in the area, the actions of governments and the demands of developers.

It may be that a school has a very small patch to develop and many children to make provision for. On the other end of the scale, some schools have vast areas of land and too few students and resources to manage it. Some schools have grown so fast that new buildings encroach upon play areas and existing gardens. One school in Brisbane lost land to developers who needed to build a stadium.

Space is a major consideration for school ground development but so too is climate, the topography of the site, style of architecture and the school history. Other factors will be the special needs of the children, teacher responsiveness to outdoor learning and budget limitations.

For reasons of diversity of sites and situations in schools, the ideas within this book are presented as a range of possibilities; a collection of imaginings, which are at times fanciful. Nevertheless, it is our hope that they will be applicable in some form in some situation.

The Designer

A schoolyard redesign is a task for the informed and many questions will need to be addressed in the process. This may not be the task of the school staff who may prefer to employ a professional designer, though input from both teacher and child is crucial in any learnscaping design.

Some key questions to be discussed;

How might the spaces be divided into areas?

- How might they relate to other spaces and the buildings
- What natural forms would be included and what built structure would be needed
- How would children and teachers use the space
- What would be the educational use of the space
- What would it provide in terms of aesthetics and stimulation
- What degree of environmental quality would it have
- What will it provide in terms of play
- How will children relate to the place
- What will it cost

The Hub

The Hub is an important and probably essential part of a design for outdoor learning. It is the outdoor gathering place for the teacher and class and the place where activities can happen or from where they can be directed. It is the homebase and it should therefore be a comfortable, sheltered place that the teacher and class like to visit.

For the purposes of this explanation I use the word 'hub' to describe this place, though it could be, The Outdoor Classroom, The Shelter Shed, The Gathering Tree or any other name that appeals. Children like to name these places. There could be one hub or multiple hubs in the grounds, all with the primary function of being a gathering place, a classroom in the outdoors, the children's other classroom.

A hub can be any structure, built or natural. In its simplest form, it is a large shady tree or a tarpaulin stretched between a few gum trees or an area covered with a shade sail. An ideal hub is a purpose-built, permanent structure.

The hub should be big enough for an entire class to be seated comfortably. The comfort factor is important and if possible, children should have a chair or bench seat to sit on. Otherwise a tarp or rug on the ground would suffice.

Voices drift in the outdoors and the hub helps keep the speaker's talk audible. It is a useful place to confine children for the first session of the activity.

Groups can disperse when they know their task and regroup in the hub when they are finished. Teachers will require no help to make full use of an outdoor classroom.

The function of the hub will depend on the type of structure erected. The more substantial the structure, the more functions are available for its use. For example, a structure with a tin or tile roof can be used to collect runoff water in a tank for use in the garden, which makes the school garden an excellent site for a hub.

A hub with a long table and bench seats becomes a workstation for any number of activities. From the messy to the fine, from art and craft, potting-on plants, to dining with music and good company.

A hub can be a shop to sell garden produce, a shelter for music practice or a place for parents to run a stall on sports day. A hub has multiple uses and if it is a comfortable place to be, teachers and children will find many good reasons to go to the outdoor classroom.

Children will want to decorate their hub with their art and craft. As an idea, use materials such as bamboo and coconut shells, twigs and twine, clay and ochres from the natural environment.

An Outdooor Classroom for every School

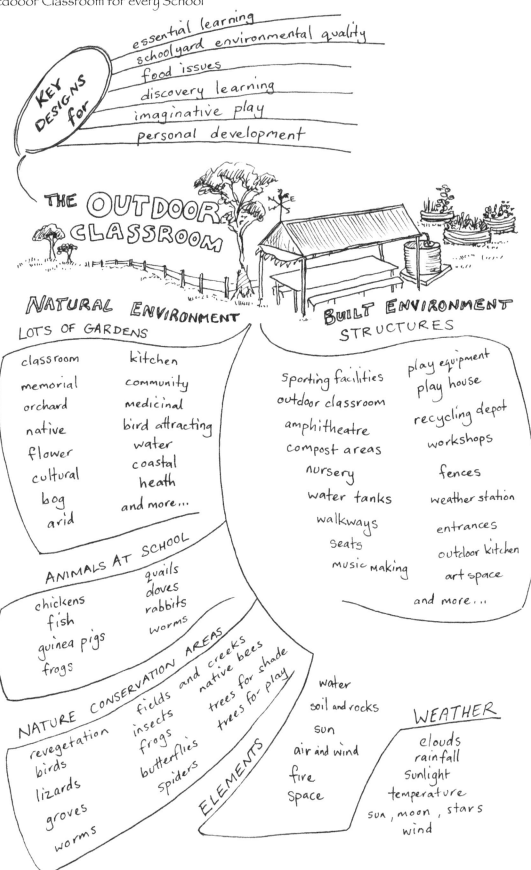

KEY DESIGNS for

- essential learning
- schoolyard environmental quality
- food issues
- discovery learning
- imaginative play
- personal development

THE OUTDOOR CLASSROOM

NATURAL ENVIRONMENT
LOTS OF GARDENS

classroom	kitchen
memorial	community
orchard	medicinal
native	bird attracting
flower	water
cultural	coastal
bog	heath
arid	and more…

BUILT ENVIRONMENT
STRUCTURES

sporting facilities	play equipment
outdoor classroom	play house
amphitheatre	recycling depot
compost areas	workshops
nursery	fences
water tanks	weather station
walkways	entrances
seats	outdoor kitchen
music making	art space
	and more…

ANIMALS AT SCHOOL

chickens, fish, guinea pigs, frogs, quails, doves, rabbits, worms

NATURE CONSERVATION AREAS

revegetation, birds, lizards, groves, worms, fields and creeks, insects, frogs, butterflies, spiders, native bees, trees for shade, trees for play

ELEMENTS

water, soil and rocks, sun, air and wind, fire, space

WEATHER

clouds, rainfall, sunlight, temperature, sun, moon, stars, wind

Working in the Outdooor Classroom

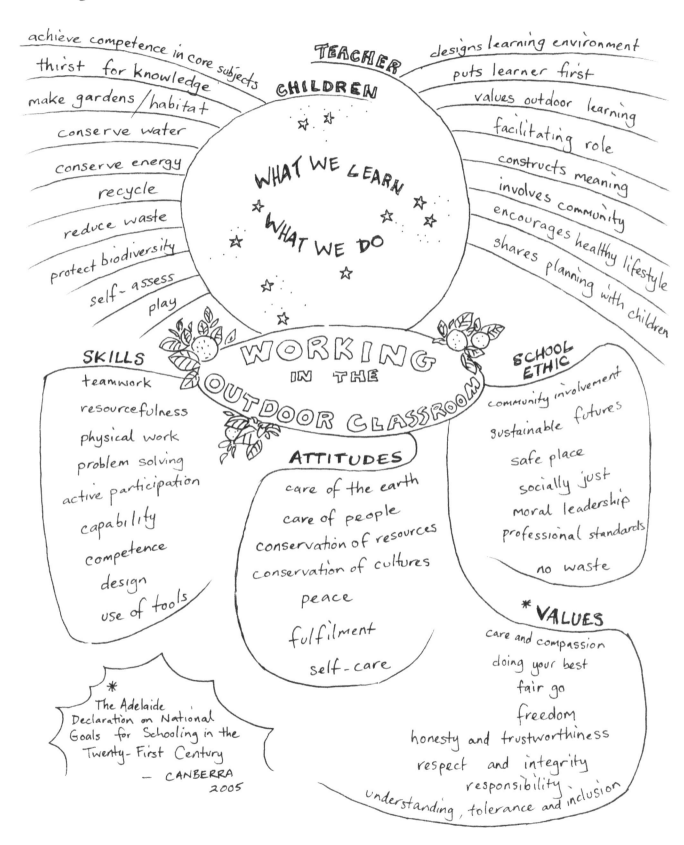

Outdoor Learning Adventures

Building on the value and benefits of the school garden and the outdoor classroom hub, we stretch the concept of outdoor learning to include designs for other learnscapes; places in the school landscape that add to the teaching resources of the school, to its naturalisation and to its play opportunities.

Not all of the following designs will pass the practical test, but view them, not as designs for implementation, but as a collection of ideas and concepts for the next stage in the development of your schoolyard. Outdoor learning is an adventure that we can embrace for better schools.

The adventures are grouped under the following headings:

- plants
- animals
- water
- soil
- rocks
- weather
- space
- landforms
- waste
- workshops
- music
- patterns
- hinden worlds
- history
- play
- signs in the garden
- jobs in the garden

Plants

Children at school learn that plants are living things, that they are flowering or non-flowering, edible or non-edible, native and non-native; that they grow in forests, woodlands, grasslands, swamps, water (fresh and salt), and in the air and that they need sunlight, water and nutrients to grow. They look at similarities and differences in plant structure, colour, shape, texture, smell, germination and seed dispersal.

It would be a great pity if children learned all this from a book without the opportunity to enter the world of real plants. A garden in the schoolground is a classroom for learning about plants. Make one, make more. Fill the nooks and crannies of the schoolyard with small gardens to work as imaginative spaces for the children to enjoy.

No plant species exists alone in nature. Animals use plants for habitat and food. Many plants need insects, birds or mammals to pollinate flowers and disperse seed. Observe this in your school garden

There is no better introduction to the world of plants than to watch a seed germinate and grow. Make a nursery in a sheltered spot in your classroom and help the kids raise plants for the garden. Plants will live happily in your classroom and if you are wild about them, you could turn your room into a living classroom like the one illustrated on page 98.

Activity – Germinate Seeds for the Garden in the Classroom

- choose big seeds as they are easy to handle: beans and peas are good
- make pots from egg cartons or rolled newspaper
- use biodegradable pots (available from shops)
- fill with seed-raising mix
- stand in a container made from the lower 10cm of a 2-litre milk container
- plant seed and water

Rainbow Garden

Geranium — RED
Nasturtium — ORANGE
Marigolds — YELLOW
Mondo Grass — GREEN
Cornflower — BLUE
Aster — INDIGO
Lavender — VIOLET

**A Garden in Every School -
A School in Every Garden**

The vegetable garden, as important as it is for children learning about food issues and healthy eating, is but one garden among a long list of gardens that could be set up in the playground.

Choose from the list or make up your own.

Children like ordered and well kept gardens but they also like gardens where they can play and feel free to touch, pick and even trample on the plants. Every school needs a wild garden where children can run around, make a cubby, hide in the grass or grab some weeds to stick in their hats.

Jackie French, author and great defender of a child's right to be free and uninhibited in the garden, suggests that plants be specially planted for such fun. Choose hardy tough plants such as lemon grass, flax, grasses and warrigal greens for ground cover. She also suggests planting groves of trees to hide under and run around.

Not all schools will have the space for wild gardens and groves, but perhaps there is space for small versions of these places.

Choose A Garden	Theme Gardens	Plants	Grow For
no-dig	pizza	vegetables	food
dig	carrot cake	medicinal	habitat
mandala	foliage	ornamentals	biodiversity
edge/border	scented	flowers	shade
circle	cottage	fodder	aesthetics
allotment	arid	native	kitchen
raised	cultural – African, Asian, Pacific, Indigenous, South American	exotic	fibre
sunken		bush tucker	play
spiral		olives	topiary
tank	alphabet	grapes	seed
container	bird attracting	grasses	cultural
narrow beds	butterfly attracting	wildflowers	community
broad beds	rainbow		
vertical growing	spikey		
trellis crops	fruit trees		
keyhole beds	vines		
water	herbs		
bog			
hedge			
bonsai			
field			
meadow			
strawbale			

Features for your Garden

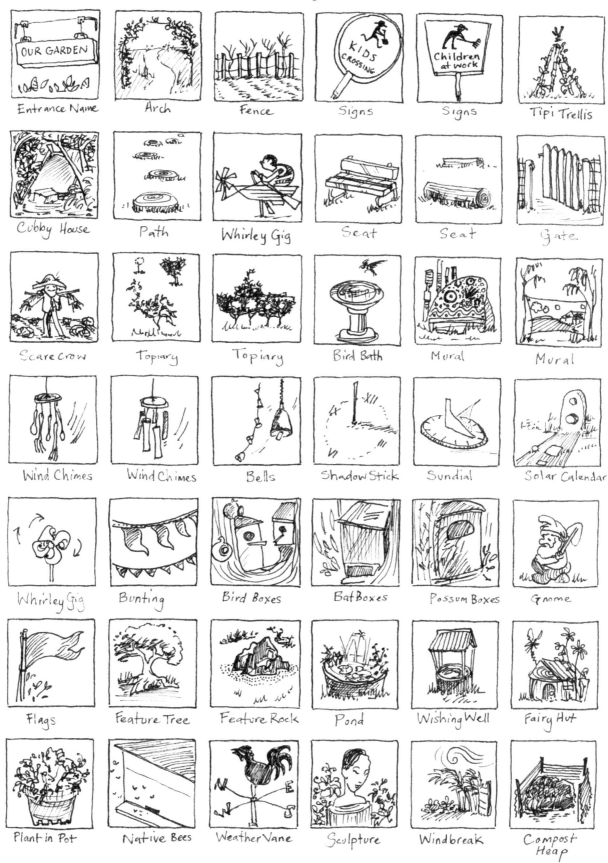

Entrance Name — Arch — Fence — Signs — Signs — Tipi Trellis

Cubby House — Path — Whirley Gig — Seat — Seat — Gate

Scare Crow — Topiary — Topiary — Bird Bath — Mural — Mural

Wind Chimes — Wind Chimes — Bells — Shadow Stick — Sundial — Solar Calendar

Whirley Gig — Bunting — Bird Boxes — Bat Boxes — Possum Boxes — Gnome

Flags — Feature Tree — Feature Rock — Pond — Wishing Well — Fairy Hut

Plant in Pot — Native Bees — Weather Vane — Sculpture — Windbreak — Compost Heap

Living Classroom

"Research has shown that people in offices respond to indoor plants in positive ways. People-Plant research shows that plants enhance productivity, reduce stress and help to induce a relaxed state of alertness."

C. Tate, Texas, 1993

Do children in a classroom respond in a similar manner to plants in their classroom?

Will information about the plants be better assimilated with the actual plant in the room? Will assimilation of non-plant information be influenced by the presence of plants in the room?

Hanging Plants   Germination of Seeds   Sprouts in jar   Bonsai   Cactus Garden
Gourds - musical instruments   Air plant   Reference Books   Terrarrium - mosses
Seed Bank   Gloves   Microscope and Slides   Mouse cage   Fountain Sculpture
Dinosaur and Volcano display   Computer   Aquarium   Mushroom Farm   Pot plants

Bush Tucker - Native Garden for your School

KEY

1 Warrigal Greens
2 Yam - Kumura Vines
3 Grass Tree + Lemon Scented Teatree
4 Native Raspberry + Sarsparilla Vines
5 Native Finger Lime
6 Grevillia + Waratah

7 Macadamia Integrifolia
8 Walking Stick + Black Palms
9 Spear Lilly
10 Bandicoot Berry
11 Davidsons Plum
12 Silver Wattle
13 Dianella + Rasp fern
14 Midgin Berry + Boobyalla

Flowers for the Teacher

A sweet scented garden planted along a pathway or against a wall will delight the senses of a child. These gardens will raise an awareness of flowers and their fragrances and the part they play in our world and in the world of other animals.

In times past, children brought flowers to school. It was a common occasion for a teacher to receive a bunch of flowers freshly picked from the home garden. It was a rare week when there was not a vase of blooms to decorate the room or a few buds twisted with silver paper to make a corsage to wear for the day and to forget to remove before shopping after school.

Times change and adults are more likely to buy their flowers today than grow them. The vase in the classroom looks to remain empty. Children could revive the floral tradition by growing flowers for the classroom.

Children can explore the many ways we and other animals use flowers. They can explore the floral language that has inspired the poet and the storyteller.

In our world, the flower expresses a language that is universally understood. In times of great happiness and in deep sadness we use the flower to express ourselves. We celebrate with bunches of flowers when the baby is born and bouquets, corsages, petals and blooms when the couple is wed. The rose speaks of love and blossoming romance and in times of sadness, we take flowers to the ill and we place them, in our grief, on the graveside.

Flowers, the temporary feature of a plant and the source of sweetness, lingers in some cases for a brief moment to be visited by an insect finding its way by its excellent sense of smell to feed, pollinate and make seed. Explore with children the plant-flower-seed cycle and save seed for the next planting.

Make a flowerbed close to the classroom for frequent visits and choose a planting theme and name for the garden. Children like rainbow gardens, fairy gardens, cottage gardens and gardens with lots of big plants like sunflowers and hollyhocks. For those with an interest in research, there is the ABC garden – A for aster B for bluebells. Whatever the garden, be it a higgledy-piggledy array of plants or a garden of roses in rows, children will enjoy this activity.

Companion Planting

All plants and animals exude gases and oils. The gardener can make good use of strong plant odours to both distract insects and allure them.

Known as selective or companion planting, a garden bed can be planted in a manner to disguise the aroma of the crop. Every moth and bug in the area will smell the school cabbages. Better to plant some garlic chives very close to them.

Another ploy for the gardener is to hide the crop. Avoid planting in rows. Better to intercrop by putting flowers and herbs amongst the vegetables.

Some Companions

- onions, shallots and chives can help protect cauliflower, kale, brussel sprouts

- strawberries love pawpaw

- tomatoes and basil, beans and asparagus

- radish and carrots

- corn and beans

Animals

The school ground can be a safe habitat for a variety of animals. Some schools are able to care for large animals such as cattle, goats, sheep, geese, ducks and the like but not all schools have a spare oval to fence to make a farmyard.

Most schools can, however, find a spot for a few chickens, a guinea pig pen, a mouse cage, pond, a rabbit hutch, a worm farm, a native beehive or perhaps a pigeon house. But all schools can increase the diversity of fauna in the schoolground by improving the environmental quality of the grounds to attract birds, lizards, insects and amphibians.

Some schools build their outdoor classroom around the needs of one animal. For example, a school in Brisbane borders on a forest that is the native habitat for a colony of koalas. The school protects this habitat and the children make a special study of this animal.

Animals will come and live in the schoolyard if the conditions are right. In some cases all they need is shelter. A pile of rocks, soil, branches and twigs will attract insects and lizards whereas the right tree or vine will attract a bird or a caterpillar looking for food.

Animals complete the ecosystem and children can learn much about their functions and products by going no further than their school ground.

Bird attracting Plants for a School Garden

Nectar
Grevillia
Callistemon
Hibiscus
Melaleuca
Hakea
Any Eucalyptus

Fruit
Walking stick Palm
Bangalow Palm
Lawyer Cane
Berries:
  Native Raspberry
  Wombat Berry
  Sarsparilla Vine
  Midgin Berry

Fruit Trees:
  Davidsons Plum
  Pawpaw
  Loquat
  Cherry Guava
  Carambola (Starfruit)
  Blue Quandong

Seeds
Spinifex Grass
Kangaroo Grass
Cane Grass
Tassel and Flag Grasses
Lomandra
Mallee Gum
Casuarina

Water
Sacred Lotus
Water Lillies
Bullrush
Pandanus

Water Provision
Bromeliads
Travellers Palm
Elkhorns
Staghorns

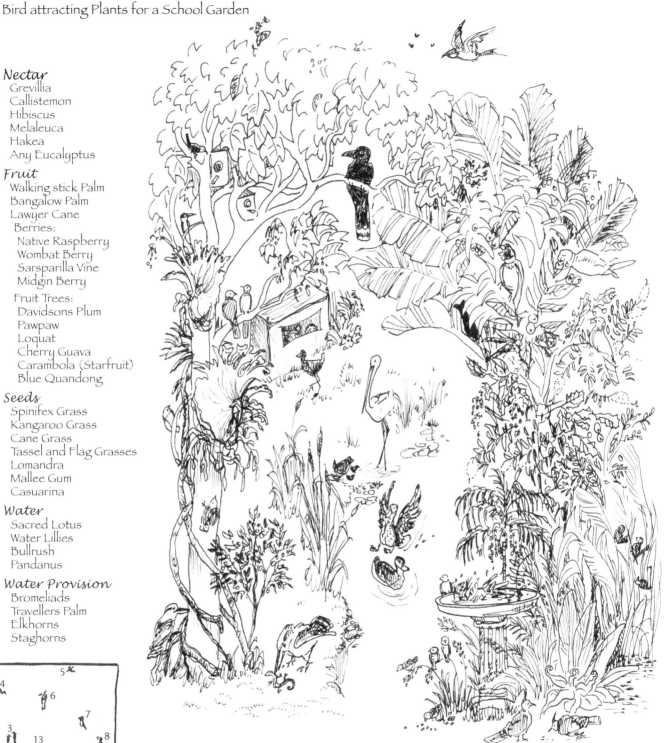

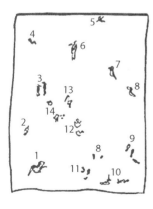

1. Kookaburra - Omnivorous
2. Rainbow Pitta - Insectivorous
3. Indian Dove - Herbivore (Fruit & seed)
4. Minor - Omnivorous
5. Bee Eater - Insectivorous
6. Kurrawong - Carnivore (Insect & Seed)
7. Rainbow Lorikeet - Fruit/ Nectar
8. Figbird - Herbivore (Fruit)
9. Finch - Seed
10. Top Knot Pigeon - Seed/ Fruit (Bangalow & Cabbage Tree Palm Seeds)
11. Blue Wren - Insect/ Seed
12. Black Duck - Omnivorous (InsecT/ Molluse Weed
13. Grey Stork - Carnivore (Snails/ Frogs/ BabyBirds
14. Water Hen/ Cock and Chick - Omnivorous

Shelters for Animals in the Schoolyard

Water for Every School

Children learn about the properties of water in their lessons at school. They learn that it is colourless, tasteless and has no smell in its purist form. They learn that it exists in three forms: liquid, solid and gas and that all living things need water. They draw diagrams of the water cycle showing water being heated by the sun over the land and sea, evaporating into clouds and condensing as precipitation. They learn about the abundance of water in the rainforests and the lack of it in the deserts and the use of water to generate electricity and today, they are learning how to save it.

Children can participate in strategies to conserve, collect, recycle and cleanse water.

Through the gardening process, children will encounter water saving techniques:

- spreading mulch to retain moisture in the soil
- slowing water run-off with ditches
- choosing water-wise plants
- auditing water use at school
- heeding water restrictions
- saving from one source to use elsewhere
- counting the number of times the water can be used

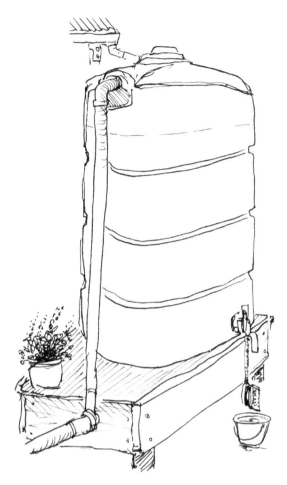

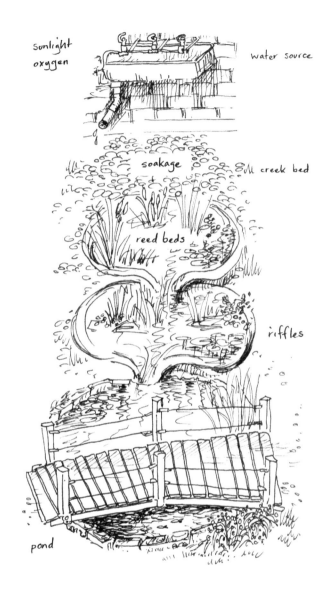

 Let children manage the water stored in a tank to learn about water conservation. The ideal tank is the one catching water from the roof of the outdoor classroom and near to the garden. A tank with a volume of 3000 litres or less would be suitable for children to manage. The mathematics of the enterprise would not elude any teacher.

Build a watercourse to demonstrate the river-to-sea movement of water over the land. Use diverted water from a drinking fountain or any other overflow.

River–to–Sea

The site is a slope with rocks laid to form a shallow creek bed. A series of ponds forms the creek, which narrows at points to make riffles for the water to run faster. Reeds planted around the edges and in the beds filter impurities in the water as it settles. The riffles oxygenate the water as it flows to the next level soaking into the soil as it moves over the slope.

It collects at the lowest point, waiting for a flow to flush it out. Small native shrubs and a bridge would complete the landscape.

The dry creek bed is a popular feature in schoolyards. Children will incorporate it into their play and teachers can use it to demonstrate that water flows in creeks only after rainfall in the drier regions of the continent.

When children begin to talk about capacity, gravity, roof capture, storage, run-off and re-use, there will be water for every school.

Water for Every School

Soil

Soil starts off as rocks which, when exposed to the harshness of the weather, crack and split making smaller rocks, which are pounded by wind and water to make even smaller rocks. Over time, these rocks are weathered into particles, which form the basis of soil.

As soils form, plants germinate, grow and die. Left behind are leaves, stems and roots, broken down by bacteria and fungi to make organic matter, which, over time, adds darkness to the soil and enriches it.

Children must delve into the science of soil to become good gardeners. They can do simple experiments to analyse the soil in their playground and this information can be used in the initial decision about where to place the garden. Not always can the garden be placed where the soil is best, so children will learn how to improve the soil in their garden and the usual way to do this is to make compost.

A Simple Soil Test

1. Collect half a jar of soil from a site.
2. Look at the colour, smell it, squeeze it and count the organisms in it.
3. Add water to the sample and leave it to settle. Organic matter will float.

The mark of a good soil for gardening:

- dark is best
- fresh earth smell is best
- adherence is good
- worms and insects are good

A pH test kit bought from a nursery or hardware shop contains a simple experiment to ascertain the soil pH, whether it is acid, neutral or alkaline. This is an appropriate activity for the older children and they could research the soil structure and pH preferred by the plants in their garden.

107

Playing in the Dirt

The earth, which nourishes the plants, also nourishes the imagination of the child who chooses to play in it. Always leave dirt areas in your garden for play. Mudpies is an age-old choice for young children. So too is playing with cars and trucks, making roads and tracks in the dirt.

If you watch carefully, the bigger kids like to get their hands dirty as well. They will add water to the dirt and build magnificent landscapes of mountains, rivers, dams and lakes. They will add roads, bridges and fences and play until the bell rings.

The older children might explore the construction of a mud-brick building; an exercise in hard physical work for youth gaining strength and ability.

Rocks

A rock is an enduring reminder of our need to find shelter, to climb to the highest point, to define our territory or just to sit to contemplate where we have been and where we are going.

Rocks hold the story of our earth from the earliest beginnings. We can see how life forms evolved from the fossils found in rocks.

Children can make a rock garden of sedimentary, igneous and metamorphic rocks, the three categories that geologists use to classify them.

We are on the third rock from the sun hurtling through space in a solar system of infinite rocks.

A rock well chosen and placed in the schoolyard can be all of the above and more to children at play.

Who is Watching the Weather?

A farmer watches the sky for rain and the flight traffic controller studies the cloud formation for the safe travel of aircraft. Those at sea watch the barometer and the surfer reads the wind and wave formations.

Begin basic weather observation at school. With a few inexpensive additions to the hardware of the schoolyard, children would have the tools to observe and record the weather. Children can learn to describe and forecast the weather when they study these elements.

Weather is made up of elements:

- temperature
- wind
- atmospheric pressure
- humidity
- clouds
- rainfall
- sunshine

Says the child to the teacher, "The barometer indicates a change in the weather is ahead and the clouds are building in the south east. They are dark and low and the wind is gathering speed. I think it will rain tonight."

Wind

Teachers have observed that the wind unsettles children and makes the school day uncomfortable. It may be a good time to take them outside to see how the wind is changing the landscape.

Wind has its function in nature and the children can see this in action. Look closely at the natural features of the landscape and note the changes. The function will depend on the temperature of the wind. Cold winds have a different effect to hot winds, but generally these effects apply:

- wind dislodges leaves, blossom and branches
- wind disperses seed and pollen
- wind cleans the air by blowing away pollutants and viruses
- wind pollutes the air by blowing in soil, smoke and other gases
- wind dries our clothes and it dries our skin, our plants, the soil and the air
- wind speed is measured by direct observation of objects in the vicinity
- trees, smoke, flags and bunting are good indicators

For more accurate descriptions of wind strength, children could check out the Beaufort Scale, an invention of Admiral Beaufort.

A wind is named by the direction from which it blows. A windsock will help children determine the direction.

The compass cardinal and half points should be on permanent display somewhere in the school ground. It can be painted on the bitumen or concrete or be atop a weather vane. Good environmental awareness begins with the understanding of simple concepts like direction. Where is north? Where is southeast?

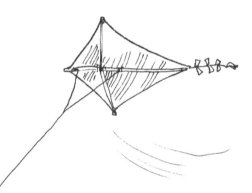

Children are well informed if they can spot from which direction the wind is blowing and what that means for the weather.

The wind can be harnessed to make electricity and one day this may happen in the schoolyard. In the meantime children can explore the wind's properties by flying a kite or building a whirligig or just hanging up bunting to brighten up the school.

Clouds

A cloud is a mass of fog, consisting of minute particles of water, often in a frozen state, floating in the atmosphere.

The study of clouds stops for many children at the level of fluffy white clouds in a blue sky for fine weather and dark clouds for rain.

The teacher can encourage the young to explore clouds to a greater depth or, maybe height, as this knowledge can aid their understanding of the weather which can then be applied in the management of their gardens.

Cloud murals around the school would help the children identify and name the various shapes.

Once they learn to observe a weather pattern, they can follow it through and learn to forecast.

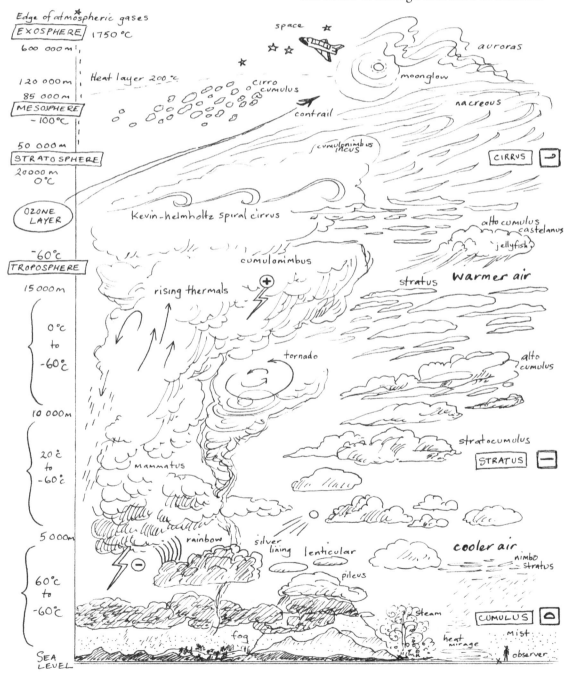

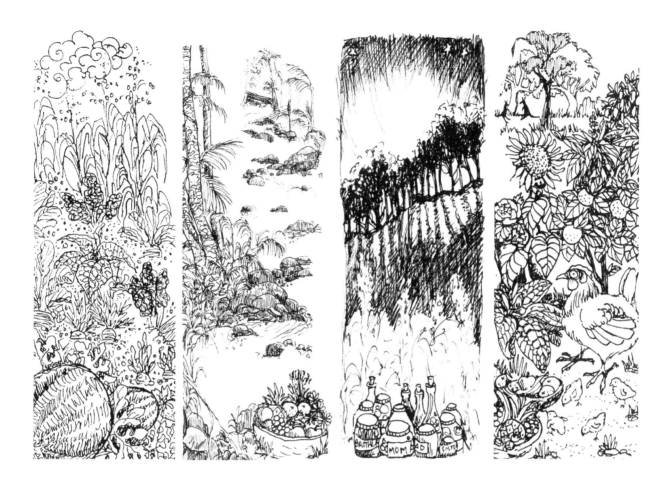

Seasons

Seasons not only affect the weather and the length of the day, they also give shape to human life.

Clothes, foods and activities vary according to the season. Since ancient times, mythologies have developed to explain the seasons. All over the world, traditional seasonal festivals and events are still celebrated. Plants and animals go through seasonal cycles.

Activities

- Plant deciduous, flowering and fruiting trees, both native and exotic, and maintain a calendar in the Outdoor Classroom to record their changes.

- Keep a calendar of seasonal weather observations.

- Prepare and eat seasonal fruits and vegetables, including those from the school garden.

- Celebrate spring with a festival.

- Research seasonal celebrations in other times and places. Why do Christmas cards show snow, and Easter cards show eggs?

- In spring, study animal behaviour in the schoolyard: nest building, insect and frog eggs, baby skinks, chrysalis building, hatching, and possums with young.

- Keep a scrapbook of seasonal sporting activities: cricket, softball, football, netball, swimming, the Melbourne Cup.

- Study the way that the position of the earth in relation to the sun causes seasons.

Space

The following is an inner solar system landscape for a primary school. It is a permanent feature in the playground and its function is twofold; to support learning in science and to be a landscape feature designed for play.

The landscape is a turfed area of the schoolyard about the size of a small classroom. Within the perimeter, in the arrangement of the inner solar system, rocks are placed to represent the Sun, Mercury, Venus, Earth and Mars.

The rocks form a play area and double as a teaching place when a class visits for a lesson on the names of the planets, their position, relative size and relationship to the Sun (some allowances here) or for any other topic in the study of space.

Children of all ages will find a use for this as a learning aid and many will find ways to incorporate it into their imaginative play and their physical fitness activity.

The outer solar system can be shown by placing markers along the 100 metre sprint track.

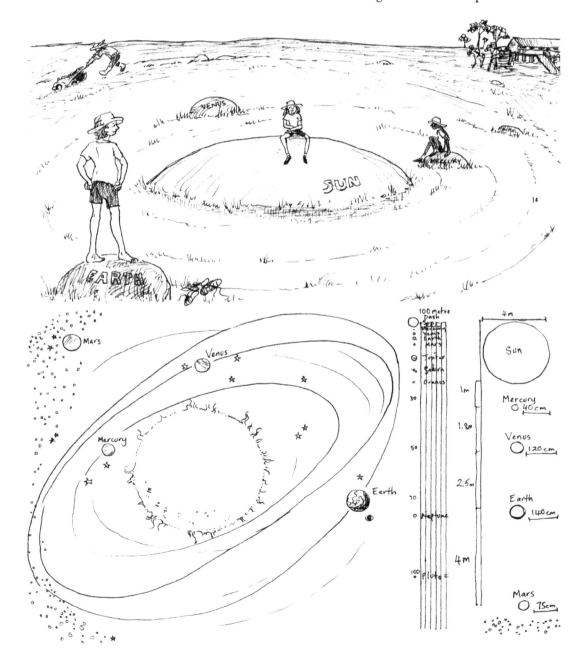

Landforms – Schoolyard Contours

Every piece of land has its own distinctive shape and is as unique as each face in a group of people. We learn about a landform by looking at it and by moving over it.

Small children learn the shapes of their landscape very well by crawling over the ground, sitting, lying, rolling and playing on it. They can remember their childhood landscapes all their lives.

A landscape is changed by the forces of nature or by human activity. Natural changes can take the form of soil erosion, landslides, earth movements such as earthquakes, or volcanic eruption. Unnatural changes include cultivation, erection of buildings and the construction of roads, rail and dams.

Activity

List all the landform features and sort them into two groups; natural or constructed. E.g.: retaining walls, drains, gullies, hillsides and garden beds. This survey might include photos, drawings, clay models and descriptions.

A dirt play area, including a hill of topsoil, enables children to experiment with constructing a landscape with roads and tunnels, dams and rivers. Toy cars and tractors help to fire the imagination. A sand pit can be used in the same way. The older children will be amused to work here.

- Do erosion experiments on hills of soil.
- Learn about contour maps, perhaps with a guest speaker from a permaculture group.
- Locate the schoolyard and its buildings on a contour map of the local district.
- Look at the symbols used for landforms on geographical maps.
- Study the schoolyard on Google Earth.
- Build a word bank of the names of natural landforms.
- Slopes, mounds, hills, valleys, gullies, cliffs, riverbeds, caves, lakes, escarpments… and more.

Produce No Waste

The categories organic and non-organic, bio-degradable and non-biodegradable, renewable and non-renewable are terms that children need to know to understand the process of recycling waste.

Waste as a concept is not limited to the 'material.' Waste also occurs in our behaviours, in our use of time and talent.

Teachers can be mindful that information too can be wasted. In other words, what we teach today may have no use in the lives of the children when they reach adulthood. This is a conundrum because we have no choice but to live in our time.

The scope of the topic is broad. Teachers who take it on may find that children will love this study because it is action-based and practical.

Recycling Ideas:

- Make compost by recycling food scraps.
- Set up worm farms.
- Make paper from waste paper.
- Learn to fix rather than discard. (Set up fix-it shops for kids for bikes/ toys/ clothes.)
- Collect water from the fountains and reuse it on the garden.
- Use waste materials in their artwork.
- Pack low waste lunches – no plastic wrap or juice boxes.
- Bring re-usable bottles and boxes.
- Support tuckshop's low waste policy.
- Design litter management strategies.
- Learn to reuse, recycle, refuse, repair and reduce.

Children, who are made aware of waste and the solutions for managing it, will recognise waste in other situations. It is an activity that links the school to home and the community.

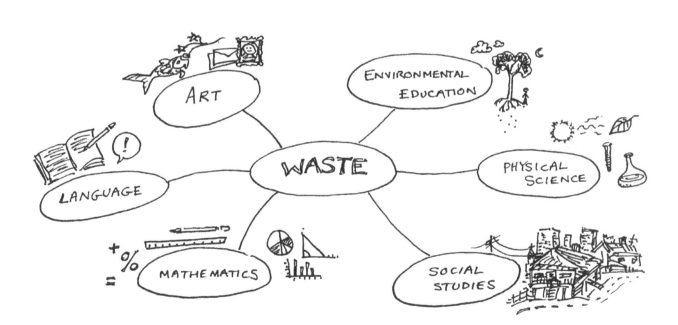

Adapted from Creative Lesson Plan on Waste
ENRE Project, DRCSC
India - 2005

The Workshop

Create workshops for children to extend their skills in construction and invention, repair and recycling.

Ideally, these would be purpose-built places to house the furniture, tools and materials that the children would need and would be staffed by a volunteer who would give freely of his or her time to run the workshops during the lunch break.

Otherwise, workshops can be set up in areas of the schoolyard, under buildings or in any available space and be supervised by teachers. Schools would need to supply the tools for the workshops and design systems to care for and store them.

Workshops	Basic Tools
The Carpenter's Shop:	Vices, hammers, small hacksaws, nails, ply
The Inventors:	Cutting tools, glue, cardboard, tape
The Bike Repair Shed:	Spanners, tube repair kits
The Recycle Shed:	Scissors, wire, board for signs
The Technology Shed:	Batteries, bulbs, solar panels, switches
The Clothes Shop:	Pins, needles, buttons, cotton, scissors
The Garden Centre:	Pots, soil, watering cans
The Paint Shop:	Paints and brushes, drop cloths, masking tape
The Mechanics Shop:	Spanners, screwdrivers, old lawnmowers

Sounds in the Outdoor Classroom

This Outdoor Classroom is used not only to study the science of sound, but also as a place to regain and practise the skill of seeking out and appreciating the sounds of the environment.

The subtleties of sound are lost to many today. Our ears are inured to lawnmowers and leaf blowers, motorbikes, television, rock music and iPod players.

Explore the sounds of nature with the children in your class.

Activities

- In the garden, provide the instruments for percussion by hanging tuned, bamboo pipes from trees or wooden frames and placing hollow logs, buckets and barrels, chimes, water-filled bottles and PVC piping where children can enjoy their music, Use them for comparing sounds, studying pitch and how it is related to size and material.

- Study vibration by the use of all the outdoor instruments, gently touching them to feel the vibrations, and grasping firmly to find how sound is stopped when we stop the vibrations.

- Study local birds and their calls, and provide a chart where children can record the time and date of hearing them in the Outdoor Classroom.

- Learn to hear and identify planes that fly overhead.

- Provide a place where students can lie still on the grass for one minute, eyes closed to sharpen the sense of hearing and talk about the subtler sounds picked up.

- Record garden sounds, then play a guessing game with them: digging, watering, sawing, pruning, snapping twigs, spreading mulch.

- Make tin-can telephones and talk about how vibrations travel.

- Find someone who can play a gum leaf and teach the children how.

The Science of Sound

Patterns

Patterns in nature are all around us. A child who can see this will understand that the world adheres to universal laws. When we give children insight into patterns, we reveal to them the secrets of the universe.

Children intuitively know these patterns as they play in the soil, making landscapes with twigs and stones. Reveal to them the evidence of those who have studied the patterns of nature and classified them.

It is one thing to look at a tree and see the whole and the parts and then to see the tree form repeated in other natural events. For example, big rivers carve deltas like branches when they join the sea and blood flows through our large arteries, branching into our veins.

Patterns are describable, repeatable, predictable and infinite in variety. They help us understand the form of the world around us, how it is shaped and what we can expect it to do.

Introduce primary school children to spirals, branching (dendritic), nets and more. Build their design skills based on patterns in nature.

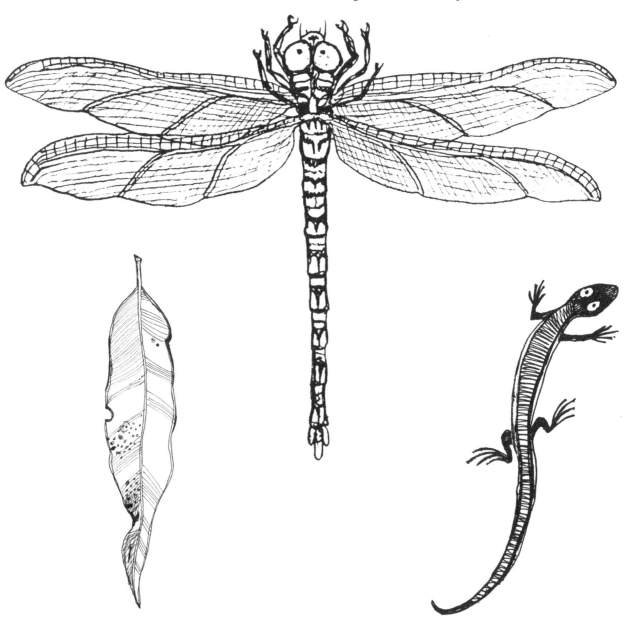

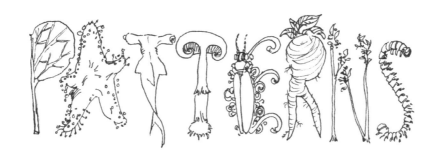

PATTERNS OCCUR IN NATURE

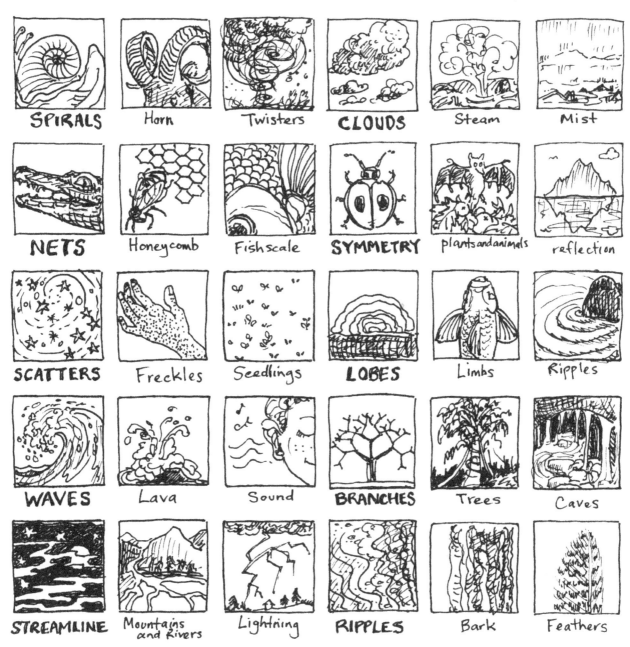

SPIRALS	Horn	Twisters
CLOUDS	Steam	Mist
NETS	Honeycomb	Fishscale
SYMMETRY	plants and animals	reflection
SCATTERS	Freckles	Seedlings
LOBES	Limbs	Ripples
WAVES	Lava	Sound
BRANCHES	Trees	Caves
STREAMLINE	Mountains and Rivers	Lightning
RIPPLES	Bark	Feathers

Palaeontology

Mock up a palaeontology dig as a fun exercise in the outdoor classroom. To include all the children in the class, more than one dig may be needed. This is an activity that older children might like to set up for a younger class.

In soft earth or sand, bury the evidence of a creature from the past that children will reveal by digging. After they have dug the site and collected all the remnant material, they can analyse it and make predictions as to the shape and size of this extinct animal. They can name it and propose what it was, what it ate, where it lived and why it died. Finish by drawing a picture of it and reporting the find to the media.

Materials to buy:

- big bones from the butcher
- teeth/ tusks
- fur or skin (leather)
- smaller bones to indicate what the animal might have eaten
- petrified wood
- remains of an aboriginal weapon such as a spearhead
- a rock with a sharp edge
- charcoal

In the Pleistocene era, dated from approximately 1.8 million to around 11,500 years ago, large megafauna including the diprotodon, a rhino-sized animal like a wombat roamed the inland areas of Australia.

The megafauna comprised a variety of animals, many now extinct. They were hunted by indigenous Australians and the fossil records tells us that they included giant crocodiles, lizards, birds, turtles, kangaroos, pythons and marsupial lions

Amateur fossil hunters, including children, can join museum groups in the search for the evidence of these vertebrates. A large number of fossils have been found in limestone caves in Naracoorte, South Australia and on the Darling Downs in Queensland.

Archaeology

Archaeologists use science, research and hard work to look for traces of the people who used the land before us. Deductions are then made about how the land was used.

In the outdoor classroom, children can be archaeologists.

Look for features of the ground that might give clues about past use, such as old drains, an indentation that might once have been a pathway, patches of concrete that might have been floors or steps or foundations, old post holes, posts or tree stumps.

- Set up a grid of pegs and string. Use spades and sieves to excavate to a certain level. Photograph and record everything found, from broken china to buttons, old coins or fencing wire.
- Find out when the school was built and research through the council library and local history resources about how this land was used before the school was built.
- Look through old photos in the school's archives. Perhaps the outdoor playground space was used for something else years ago, such as a rose garden, the school pine forest, the old outdoor toilets or the horse paddock.
- When there is a school anniversary, teams of students might interview past pupils about the use of the schoolyard in their time.
- Use library books to study the way archaeologists have worked to uncover past civilisations, including those in Australia.

The Gold Rush

Give a child a role to play, a story to tell, a costume and some props and the events of history will unfold in the classroom and be a lasting reminder for all the children.

Classrooms can be too small for epic productions so a move into the outdoors may be in order. Choose a grassy knoll with a few trees nearby to tie the painted backdrop and a flat area to set up the props and tent. The stage is set for 'The Gold Rush,' a play by Year 5.

A digger leaves the gold fields pushing a wheelbarrow containing a pick and shovel. He is depressed, penniless, out of luck and on his way back to Melbourne. He has not found a speck of gold. He comes upon a happy young man heading for the field. They stop and talk and a price is agreed upon for the wheelbarrow and tools…

When the mood is set and the energy of the outdoors comes into play, children will bring the drama to life. They will make up the dialogue as they go and their teacher will know by their knowledge of the times how effective the teaching has been.

The outdoor set-up for staging small classroom plays can be simple and inexpensive. There is an advantage in having some structure, as children will use the place in their playtime if they identify it as a playhouse. Voices drift in the outdoors so a solid backdrop has the advantage of better sound. The end wall of a low set building is ideal for this purpose and if a raised awning can be attached to form a roof, then the acoustics will be better still. This may be all that the school needs to do to make a very adequate outdoor playhouse for children.

Historical Stories to act out in the outdoors

- Landing of the First Fleet in Port Jackson
- The Indigenous Australians
- The Timber Getters
- Government in Australia – three tiers
- Pioneers

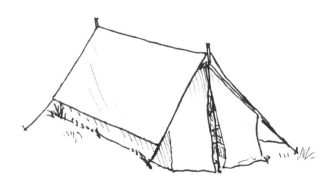

Things Children Like to do Outside

Quiet Nook · Hug a Tree · Sculpture · Flax Corridor · Maze · Rope Ladder

Swing · Swing · Animals · Bird Hide · Marbles · Tower

Running Water · Rocks · Territories · Mud pies · Stepping Stones · Dreamcatcher

Play House · Meadow · Climb fences · Places to Run · Hopscotch · Pathways

Leaf Skeletons · Hide + Seek · Tracking Mini-beasts · Tadpoles · Paddle Pop Stick Trail Messages · Mandala

Toy Cars in Dirt · Sandpit · Dams · Weeds to pick · Flowers to pick · Tipi Cubbyhouse

Gunyah · Bridges · Domestic Animals · Follow Insects · Buried Treasure · Cloud Watching

The Play Platform

The play platform is a small deck-like structure 1000mm x 1200mm and raised 200 - 300 millimetres off the ground. The size and shape can vary but a small platform will encourage the imaginative play of 2-3 friends. It is a simple structure that will sit unobtrusively in the garden until a child decides that it is the floor of a cubby or a stage for a concert. If it is placed near to the classroom, teachers will put it to good use as well.

The design works on the principle that less is more. A simple structure is sufficient to inspire children to create imaginative scenarios. They will set the scene with props found on the ground around them, or brought from home or the classroom, and play until the bell rings.

A roof on the platform is an added feature that will suggest other uses for the platform and if a wall is added with a cut-out window to look through, they will have a puppet theatre or a shop.

The platforms can be set up anywhere but close to the classroom is best. The openness of the design will help teachers supervise the children at play. Some schools will need to think about shade and protection from the sun and may choose to install the structure under a tree or sail. Some platforms may need regular checking for spiders where they are plentiful.

This platform has the potential to create problems in the playground if there is only one and the demand is high. Overcome this by building several, preferably out of sight of each other or develop other play areas with equal appeal.

Special School Gardens for Play

- dirt
- dinosaur
- flowers to pick
- weeds
- grasses
- wildflowers
- tree circles
- flax runs
- climbing trees
- groves
- secret

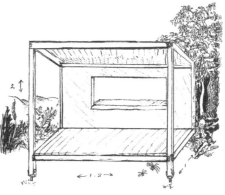

Dinosaur Forest for Play and Study
Jurassic Period 208 to 144 million years ago

KEY

1 Billy's Buttons	7 Bromeliad
2 Prickly Rasp Fern	8 Ginko Biloba Tree
3 Bush Iris	9 Rough Tree Fern
4 Walking Stick Palm	10 Wollemi Pine
5 Bird's Nest Fern	11 Papyrus Reed
6 Elkhorn Fern	12 Sacred Lotus

Signs for the Garden
See page 174 for more ideas

Playground Markings

Playground markings are an excellent way for schools to increase the play opportunities for children, provide useful information that can be on permanent view and improve the ambiance of areas around the classrooms.

Traditionally, we see markings for hopscotch and handball, clock faces and counting ladders etc on the hard surfaces around the school. These are mostly reproductions of the markings children made for themselves before playgrounds were covered with grass and asphalt. In recent years, schools have added new designs to their playgrounds and have chosen, on the whole, bright colours to appeal to the children.

Markings can provide useful curriculum resources for teachers. Try a few mathematical markings or symbols, such as infinity, male, female, cloud shapes, compass points, directional signs, up, down, punctuation marks, traffic signs, chemical abbreviations and the like. They can be useful teaching tools but they should not overpower the play areas. Design well, consider the needs of the teachers and children and find an artist or signwriter to do them.

Schools wishing to move play onto softer surfaces could expose an area of dirt for children to make their own markings or they could mark the grass, as seen on running tracks.

Children are learning all the time.

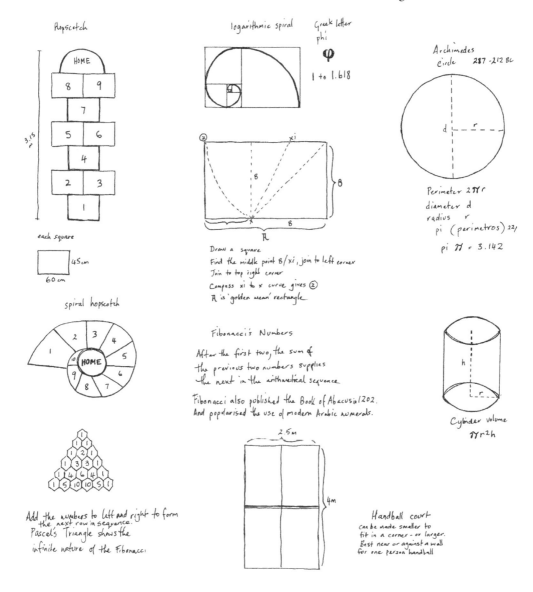

Jobs for Children in the School Garden

Work in the school garden involves much more than the physical work of the gardener. The skills needed extend beyond the planting, watering and harvesting. They include the work of the researcher, the scientist, the conservationist, the designer, the seed saver to name a few. Teachers can allocate these jobs to the children, giving each a special role in which to develop some skill and knowledge through their own resources. (Two children might like to share one job.)

The child, for example, who is in charge of security, might be the person who checks that the garden gate is closed or locked each day and that the produce is not being picked before it is ready. The soil scientist can learn to use the pH soil testing kit and report when the soil needs adjusting or fertilising. These children would be encouraged to think about their role and be pro-active in its design. The potential for learning in such a situation would not be lost to the teacher.

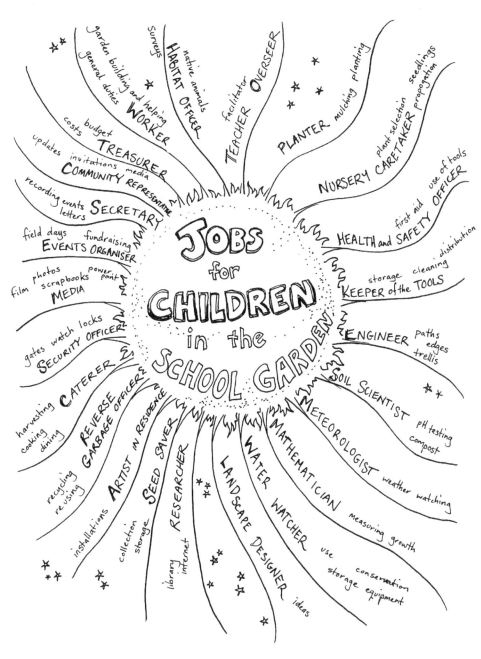

Part IV

Curriculum connections
Linking school gardens to curricula

Curriculum Connections

For the teacher looking for the links between the garden and the curriculum, we can start by delving way back into human history, when the tillage of the earth marked the very beginning of civilisation.

Around 10 000 years ago when the Neolithic people grew seed in the moist soil of the river valleys and at the edges of lakes, the first farmers appeared. Anthropological studies suggest that women made up the mass of early farmers and they planted wheat and barley seed that they had carried from the once fertile valleys of the Middle East to these shrunken valleys and lakes. A long, cold dry period that was to last 1000 years caused a dramatic climatic change and the cultivation of the seed was an act of survival. It was also an act that was to change what 'being human' meant.

The early acts of civilisation occurred at reasonably simultaneous times in history within regions across a common latitude of the earth. The Chinese in Asia and the Aztecs, Mayan, and Incas in the Americas, and in the southern hemisphere, in the highland valleys of the Papua New Guinea interior where it is understood the root crop, taro, was extensively cultivated.

In time, science, literature and the fine arts unfolded as a high degree of civilisation was attained. Horticulture, the cultivation of vegetables, fruits and ornamental plants, became the pursuit of the civilised man. A sensibility emerged that the simple garden was a connection with nature and with the beauty of the landscape. Devotion of time and care to a garden was seen as enriching and gratifying and, in essence, part of a civilised life.

From all points in our history, knowledge has accumulated and been ordered into discrete subjects which form the content of the modern curriculum.

The scientific relations of horticulture are extensive and the connection to the modern curriculum is in the branches of science, natural history, physics, botany, minerology, chemistry, and hydraulics and to the fine arts through art, architecture and literature.

When we turn to the garden, we enter the cradle of knowledge and the search for the connections to the curriculum is without effort. The curriculum is in the garden and the garden is in the curriculum. They are one and the same.

What is Curriculum?

Curriculum is the course of study as outlined by the educational authorities. It is the intentional provision made by educators to support children's learning. What we teach in schools is given and teachers have a legal obligation to teach what the authorities set down.

Each state in Australia provides a curriculum for their schools and this situation has given rise to discussion of a national curriculum - one curriculum to serve all states. The federation of curricula may be introduced in the near future but at this point the states retain control. The argument for national curricula focuses strongly on the need for children moving from state to state to experience uniformity in their education. There are other reasons for streamlining the provision of education that have to do with issues of economics and practicality, and to be hoped, better schools.

A curriculum is not static. It is constantly being renewed and teachers will experience many changes in curricula over a career in teaching. Some curricula have a longer shelf life than others but change is in the nature of things, it happens and we adapt.

> Children learn things at school that are not set out in the curriculum and this is often referred to as the 'hidden curriculum' or 'incidental learning.' Children are learning all the time.

Whatever the dialogue - be it key learning areas, core curriculum, education for sustainability, new basics, essential learnings, current curriculum - the role of teachers is to work within the set guidelines.

Where Choice Lies

While there may not be choice about the work itself, there is always a choice about the way teachers do their work. Teachers exercise this choice every day when they design a lesson. Herein lies the essence of the teacher's work. S/he has the freedom to choose the learning environment, to design the teaching and learning task, to select a teaching strategy, to gather resources and to be creative in the process.

The teacher can choose where children learn, in the classroom, at a desk, on the floor, on the veranda, at the local shopping centre, in a garden or at the zoo. S/he can decide when the children will learn something - morning or afternoon, this week or next and which topics to teach from the syllabus. There is also choice about how children will learn and which learning style will be chosen for the topic. Most teachers base their decisions on their view of what is best, considering the circumstances.

The world of teaching may not be so simple for some teachers. The freedom of the teacher to act alone is somewhat restricted when schools have a policy that requires teachers working in the same year level to plan together and work on the same program. This uniformity may work well for efficient, time-saving planning and may be effective in securing accountability and assessment goals such as the results for the moderation committees, but it would appear to be seriously restricting for the teacher who has a good idea half way through the program run.

Teachers need their good ideas for effective teaching, and while they can take their best thoughts to the year level planning meetings, they may be unsuccessful in having them accepted.

To lose the option to work independently must be a serious restriction in the teaching task. To give up this mode, to replace it with attendance at multiple meetings, to navigate through the personalities of your colleagues in the quest for a decision, must be the ruin of many a good teacher. It is to be hoped that teachers never lose their control over their design of the learning environment.

The Garden in the Curriculum

When teachers choose the garden as a resource for teaching the curriculum, they are making a personal choice about the way they want to work. Gardening will not be the choice of all teachers. Children benefit by being in a school where there is diversity, where the teacher is free to develop teaching strategies based on their particular expertise, interest or special skill - be it gardening, photography or macramé.

The value of any resource is in its efficacy and the garden, as a resource, has a collection of attributes that make it a valuable resource for any school. Its value lies in the nature of what a garden is.

A garden is many things, but in a school setting, it is a natural environment that can be transformed into an outdoor classroom and here, just as in the indoor classroom, learning occurs, albeit it in a different form.

Teachers are resourceful. Everyday, they build rich images of the world for their students through the creative use of resource materials and their own knowledge. They work in their classrooms, using all the available nooks and crannies, vertical and horizontal spaces, multiple rearrangements of furniture to create a bright and interesting learning environment for the children.

But the classroom, while being an indispensable site for learning, has constraints and limitations as a site.

These restrictions can be somewhat overcome by moving outside, that is, beyond the veranda into the schoolyard, adopting the view that the grounds are an existing and available resource, that, if developed, would increase, by extension, the overall learning area available to the teacher.

The creation of natural and built areas in the school ground is to utilise a resource that has been largely overlooked in recent times. There is good sense in making the indoor and outdoor classrooms a package for all teachers. It may be that the modern urban child needs both classrooms to rock their world into balance.

What We Know

The act of planting a seed draws on knowledge from many subjects: soil science, botany, hydrology, horticulture, mechanics, mathematics, microbiology, bio-genetics and meteorology to mention a few, maybe art and spirituality as well. Work in the garden cannot be other than multi-disciplinary. Traditionally separate subject disciplines are integrated in the practical world.

We need subject classifications to avoid chaos in our thinking but children's learning need not be locked to this. Classifications are dissolved in the real world and the teacher who supervises the planting of the seed may need, for the purposes of documentation, to choose if it is a science activity in propagation or a maths lesson in measurement, or an English lesson in reading instructions. It will be the teacher's task to identify the syllabus to which the activity belongs - in other words, the curriculum link.

The Multi-disciplinary Resource: The School Garden

The activities of a school garden can be integrated into the classroom in many ways. Typically it enters the curriculum as a resource for teaching science – for lessons on plant life and insect behaviour for example, but a garden at school can be much more. With a little resourcefulness, the activities of the school garden can be applied to just about any lesson taught in the classroom.

From literacy to craft, from maths to health and studies in society, learning in the garden draws from all areas of the curriculum. The information on a packet of seeds, for example, exemplifies the breadth and scope of a growing activity as a curriculum exercise. The information applies to lessons in maths (depth, width, height), to studies in society (climatic zones), to language (instructions and vocabulary building), geography (mapping) and, typically, the science lessons (plant growth, seasons, weather and the water cycle).

Gardens have inspired artists for all time and children who have a deep connection to their garden may be moved to write a poem or read a story in the garden. A garden can be a setting for a musical event or a site for the installation of art works made from the sticks and stones of the schoolyard. Gardens will satisfy the creative spirit of children, and teachers will see without looking, ways to capture their creativity in the garden.

> *"Gardens work as imaginative spaces – on the ground as well as in words and pictures. They relate to the world beyond their walls and fences."*
>
> Stephen Deuchan

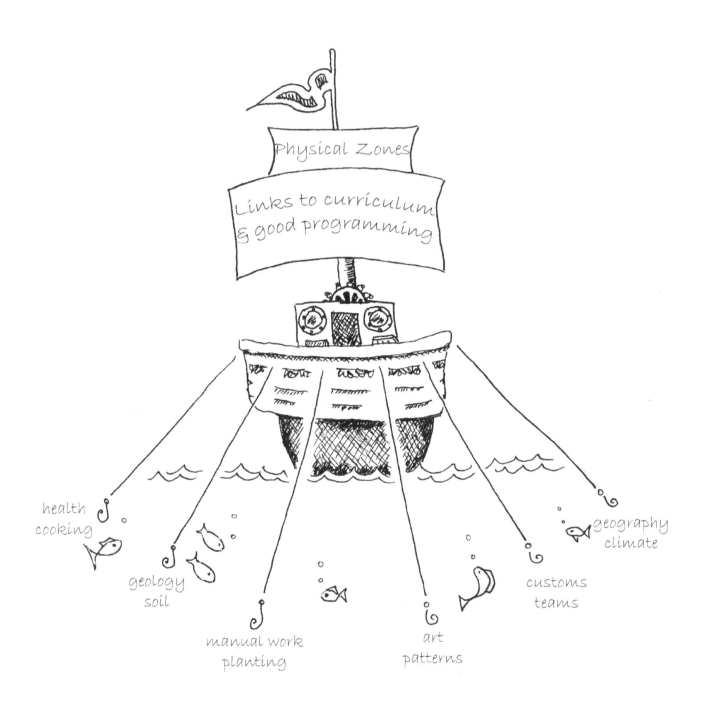

Linking School Gardens to Curricula

Once some teachers have shown interest in the garden and there is confidence in expanding its use, then it is time to explore the full potential of outdoor classrooms.

The school garden and learning outdoors can be of most value to teachers and students by providing opportunities for hands-on, relevant and authentic experiences that present concrete examples of the learning that routinely occurs within the classroom.

Teachers put a great deal of effort into developing programs that:

- meet the curricula demands as set down by their education department
- fit with the school vision and goals
- prepare students to take their place in the local community and in the wider society
- engage students in meaningful activities
- are possible within the constrains of
  resources
  time allocations
  and class size
- reflect the level of skills and knowledge of the students and the teacher

With so many factors, all of which change and evolve over time, it is easy to see why teachers can feel that they simply can't fit another thing into the school week or into their programming workload, notwithstanding learning a new set of garden skills.

But teachers are also looking for ways to make their lessons interesting, meaningful and memorable. It is the satisfaction of having successful learners that is generally the real reward for the teacher.

When children are engaged, happy and learning, if their progress is demonstrable, recordable, reportable, if the learning is at their appropriate stage of development or beyond, in activities that instill values that the community deems worthy, then that is the aim of all teachers and all policy. It is helpful to view the various 'demands' as guidance and support while seeing the difficulties of the task as the rationale for using the school garden.

Involving the school garden into school lessons throughout the curriculum can often be made easier by changing the way programs are expressed and the way assessment and reporting is conducted.

You may be a classroom teacher, the principal, or a school garden consultant; providing you have some understanding of teaching, programming and believe in the possible benefits of school gardens, you can facilitate the following workshops.

Staff Workshops that Lead Teachers Through the Process to Involve the Garden with Curricula.

Workshop 1

Part 1

Ask your staff what they want a child to have gained by being at your school. The statements in reply will usually be sweeping, global statements such as:

- preparedness for a challenging future
- an ability of the children to learn in and from different situations throughout their life
- enjoying the learning process
- being engaged in the learning activities
- having good self-esteem
- caring for others
- having fond memories of their childhood and school
- having the skills and the tools to be able to be successful (in all the senses of the word)

These statements should reflect the School Vision Statement but all you need to do at this time is to revisit the ideas quickly to personalise them.

Now point out the links between these statements and department of education policy. This will be really valuable if there are new policies that some of the staff may be struggling with. It is reassuring to teachers to realise that their goals and perceptions are also those at the core of all government education policy.

If this session goes well, teachers will be feeling more like capable professionals than slaves to policy. Improving self-esteem raises confidence and creativity.

The next part of this workshop is an exploration of possible benefits to linking the garden to the curriculum.

Part 2

Make clear to the participating teachers, that the brainstorming that follows is the *exploration of potential* at this point and that any adoption of a plan or policy will be another decision for another time.

Now you need to set about showing that activities in and about the school garden can promote and/ or affect favourably any of the global statements about the outcomes of schooling you, your staff, the community and government can make.

Go back to the vision statements in Part 1 and link each one with the garden.

Your brainstorm may have similar results to the following;

> *Preparedness for a challenging future*

Operating in nature, systems thinking, everybody has to eat, cost of food in the future, self reliance, clean healthy food, healthy weight adults, local production, slow food movement, organic food, nutrition

> *The ability of children to learn in and from different situations and to use this skill throughout their lives*

Life-long learning, learning from a variety of adults, understanding how to learn from others, meeting the needs of learners in learning styles, seeing and doing, many aspects to become interested in (soils, water, nutrition, processing etc), transfer knowledge from one situation to another, diversity keeps interest high, more engaged learners

> *Enjoying the learning process*

Adds variety to the day, gets the kids moving, opportunity to show a wide range of skills not used in classrooms, improved self-esteem for the non-academic, providing activities that have a direct outcome and purpose, good for the kinesthetic learners

> *Being engaged in the learning activities*

More opportunities to cater for individual learning styles, using the skills from the classroom work in real situations, having children move around and handle things, taking the interest from the garden back into the classroom

> *Having good self-esteem*

Opportunities for the less academic student, caters for children who find it difficult to sit still for long periods, can be more child centred, links school with activities from home that children can share with peers

> *Caring for others*

Leads to the understanding of the basic needs of all mankind, understand the work involved in food production, shows the value of diversity, need to care for all species

> *Having fond memories of their childhood and school*

Child centred activities, a lot of group work, sense of achievement, gardening is the most common leisure time activity

> *Having the skills and the tools to be able to be successful (in all the senses of the word)*

Develop generic skills, self confidence, self-reliance, understanding systems, developing systems thinking, produce a product

> *"How is it that a garden can be such a valuable learning tool?*
>
> *The world is a garden and all human activity is about meeting our needs within the universal laws of our environment."*
>
> Janet Millington 2006

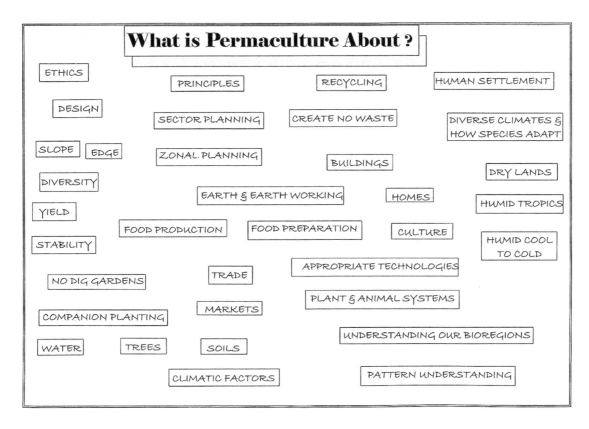

What is Permaculture About?

ETHICS · PRINCIPLES · RECYCLING · HUMAN SETTLEMENT · DESIGN · SECTOR PLANNING · CREATE NO WASTE · DIVERSE CLIMATES & HOW SPECIES ADAPT · SLOPE · EDGE · ZONAL PLANNING · BUILDINGS · DRY LANDS · DIVERSITY · EARTH & EARTH WORKING · HOMES · HUMID TROPICS · YIELD · FOOD PRODUCTION · FOOD PREPARATION · CULTURE · HUMID COOL TO COLD · STABILITY · NO DIG GARDENS · TRADE · APPROPRIATE TECHNOLOGIES · COMPANION PLANTING · MARKETS · PLANT & ANIMAL SYSTEMS · WATER · TREES · SOILS · UNDERSTANDING OUR BIOREGIONS · CLIMATIC FACTORS · PATTERN UNDERSTANDING

Workshop 2

Part 1

Once teachers see that there is value in incorporating the school garden into the curriculum, then the very next step is to show them just how much is already done in the classroom that is essentially about the outdoors.

Here is a chart showing many of the things that permaculture is about. It may be used as it is, or modified if your staff does not want the broader scope permaculture offers.

Take a moment to look at the chart and you will begin to see the potential links for yourself. You may even start to write in those topics, themes or units of work that can go with the headings.

Then present the blank chart to the staff.

For a staff meeting, flashcards and butchers paper or projection onto a white board may help. Designate a colour pen to each grade and ask them to write in what they already do under these headings. It won't take long to fill up a board with science and human culture related topics.

Then return to the chart and ask teachers to find real-life activities in mathematics under each of the headings. You will be surprised at the diversity and creativity of the responses such as:

- graphing
- using the basic operations in calculating;
  - size
  - amount
  - volume
  - weight
- problem solving
- budgeting
- angles of slope
- calculating height through triangulation
- creating a right angled corner
- categorisation
- set theory
- number patterns
- number series such as the Fibonacci Series

The list can be expanded to include more detail but stop when it is clear that garden activities can give real life experiential links to mathematics.

Now return to the chart and ask teachers to list all of the writing genres that could be incorporated into the topics. They will find that they can list all the genres and your list will include but will not be limited to the following:

- creative writing
- letters
- research
- reports
- poetry
- memos
- lists

Once again stop when they get the picture.

Then ask them to note all the reading opportunities. These will flow very easily and so in a short time you have demonstrated that the school garden can be a learning resource in all the basic subjects.

Make this point clearly:

We have just shown that by giving children experiences in the garden and related to the garden, we can make learning in all the basic subjects more real, meaningful, enjoyable and memorable.

If time permits, your staff may wish to continue to find links with the creative arts, and then move to physical education and health. The garden is also about the physical work and gardening which requires strength, to improve flexibility, agility and an understanding of fresh clean healthy food and so then you can make the added point:

We have just demonstrated that by adding authentic activities in the outdoors that we can address learning in all the Key Learning Areas.

At this point most teachers will see the potential to make the key learning areas more real and meaningful, but they may not yet be convinced that the work to set up the garden and link it to the curriculum is worth the effort.

Part 2

Now you ask them this important question.

"What do we need to do to improve those things we are not doing well, or could do better at this time?"

Put this question to small groups to list problems or obstacles to learning that they have identified in their classrooms or across the whole school. (The group work allows individuals some anonymity as comments may be seen as criticism).

The responses will be some or all of the following:

- some or many students are not engaged in the learning activities
- low motivation
- inability to focus on a task
- inappropriate and/or unacceptable behaviours
- non academic students having low self-esteem
- bullying
- short attention spans
- children at different levels of development in the basic subjects
- disconnectedness with the community
- not having good flow of work from one grade to the next and repetitions of themes and topics
- little variety of assessment situations that show transfer of learning from one situation to another
- lack of parental support
- low teacher satisfaction
- pressure of new government policy

As we all well know, there will be many more that crop up from time to time. Problems will come and go depending on the culture of the school, the educational climate and societal changes. Teachers will always have things they want to do better. The issue and the degree of the problem will come out of the special circumstances of each school and in each classroom.

Now you have a list of things that in most cases can be addressed to some degree by expanding the learning activities into the outdoors.

Part 3

Explore each problem and ask teachers to suggest approaches and activities that could work towards reducing or eliminating the problem with particular reference to outdoor activities and the school garden. Solutions may directly or indirectly involve the garden.

Combining the learning opportunities of the garden with its potential to solve some otherwise difficult problems can be quite powerful in motivating teachers to explore the possibility of planning to move some learning into the outdoors.

Your list may look like this;

◎ *Some (to many) students are not engaged in the learning activities*

Varying the activities and the venue can give students a new perspective, non-academic students have a chance to excel, hands-on learners will see more meaning in the learning activities.

◎ *Low motivation*

Looking forward to special time outdoors can motivate students to complete class work quickly. Having a real situation to think about, plan, calculate and report on can stimulate interest that would otherwise be difficult to arouse and sustain.

◎ *Inability to focus on a task*

Varying activities will continually stimulate interest. Moving physically can dissipate energy that can build up in children forced to sit for long periods.

◎ *Inappropriate and/or unacceptable behaviours*

The garden can be used as an incentive and a reward. Many children find moving outside easier than working at a desk. Pressure from peers for good behaviour, so the class can go and stay outside.

◎ *Non-academic students having low self-esteem*

Create a wider range of opportunities for students to show their abilities. Valuing outside work can open vocational prospects for children who do not do well in class.

◎ *Bullying*

Creating places for creative play in breaks reduces the boredom of playtime that may lead to finding inappropriate entertainment. Raising the self-esteem of the under achievers will reduce their need to show power over the higher achievers. Creates the opportunity for children to develop respect for the diversity of the garden as well as in human abilities.

◎ *Short attention spans*

Children can stay on task longer if the activity holds meaning for them. Diversity in lessons increases participation and engagement.

◎ *Children at different levels of development in the basic subjects*

Can help in composite classes allowing each group to share a central theme but working at different skills' levels. Bridges the gap between the achievement levels across the basic subjects.

◎ *Disconnectedness with the community*

Can involve the parents and the wider community. Can be a joint project between staff, children and parents. Many parents want to be involved in the school but are not confident with helping in the academic subjects. School can show it is a place of learning for all ages and offer gardening workshops.

◎ *Not having good flow of work from one grade to the next and repetitions of themes and topics*

Can be a focal point to review and revive planning documents as part of whole school planning. The huge variety of topics from the outdoors can be used to work with children on the one activity but at different levels.

◎ *Little variety of assessment situations that show transfer of learning from one situation to another*

Assessment in the outdoors allows teachers to observe and record the transfer of skills and knowledge from the classroom into practical applications in the outdoors.

◎ *Lack of parental support*

Allows another mode of engaging parents.

◎ *Low teacher satisfaction*

Increases opportunities for teachers to provide exciting activities for the children. Child-centred learning can open up new professional opportunities for teachers who allow the children to direct the learning so that the teacher becomes the facilitator and not the expert.

Now state this conclusion:

Working in the garden can help us make learning more relevant and fun in all the KLAs and it may even save us time by minimizing some of the problems we have that blocks or slows down learning.

Part 4

This activity is to find all the possible ways that the garden establishment and ongoing maintenance can be supported and what tools, templates or methodologies may make programming easier.

Brainstorm the question, *"Who might support us in the garden set-up and maintenance?"*

Most likely you will get responses such as these;

- ◎ parents (perhaps some specific names)
- ◎ the P & C
- ◎ the local garden club
- ◎ conservation groups
- ◎ the local permaculture group
- ◎ council
- ◎ local schools that already have gardens
- ◎ the school garden network
- ◎ special ethnic community groups
- ◎ department of health
- ◎ after school care
- ◎ holiday care
- ◎ local garden suppliers

Then ask what would make programming easier. The suggestions will be along the lines of:

- ◎ sharing the ideas
- ◎ seeing how other schools have done it
- ◎ planning across the grades
- ◎ using prepared planning templates
- ◎ pupil free day for planning

Ask teachers to sum up the amount of help available and if that would help them support a school garden.

If the section goes well then you can ask teachers if they would like to further explore using the garden and the outdoors as it appears that it may;

- ◎ be a different way to present the skills and knowledge we have always taught
- ◎ solve some of our problems at the same time
- ◎ not increase preparation time after the initial set up

If they stop discussion at this time it is not necessarily a bad outcome. You will have stimulated some thinking and hopefully you will have led some of your staff to understand gardening can be just gardening but at the same time it can be the way to provide hands-on learning and give practical expression to classroom work.

Even if they decide to explore the concept more fully, don't ask or expect all teachers to leap on board and be outside with their classes straight away or regularly. As discussed in previous chapters, the decision to move outside cannot be taken lightly and only the classroom teacher will know the correct time to involve students in outdoor learning activities. But if the garden is already established, then it can be brought into the class-work as concrete examples, or to illustrate a point, well before the class visits it in lesson time.

Some teachers may like to begin by incorporating the garden into a lesson here and there or have a special day set aside. Some may even plan weeks of work based on the garden; the planting, the growing, harvesting and even preparing or marketing the produce.

These are good results but ones that do not go all the way to ensure the ongoing viability of the garden. Staff may transfer out of the school and if the main garden users leave, then the whole garden/ curriculum process has to be done all over again.

Aim for a Whole School Plan

A decision to undertake a whole school planning process is the best result from the staff workshops.

If successful in Workshops 1 and 2 then wait for the right time to move towards the next few sessions that will explore the planning and implementation of a whole school garden plan.

Because of the diversity of circumstances, situations and resources in each school, you need to select an approach, or a combination of approaches, that will suit your particular needs. There will already be other models or you may invent your own, but the following approaches have worked in schools that have very different circumstances, and are offered to you through the generosity of time and spirit of the staff members who have been through the process.

These approaches may be put to the staff or more usually, the principal and key school garden enthusiasts, who are able to quickly identify the one that best suits their school community.

Workshop 3

This workshop is to introduce the selected approach to the staff and to work towards the establishment of a whole school planning approach to the school garden. The approach should be described to staff and they should be told that after the next workshop they will be asked whether or not the school should begin work on a whole school plan to incorporate the garden into the curriculum. This gives them a while longer to wish and dream without making a commitment.

Here are some approaches to discuss along with any others you have heard of or have designed.

Approach 1

One Major Subject for Each Year

Some schools will design a plan allocating a specific aspect of the garden to a special year. In this plan, although the children are involved in the garden throughout their schooling, one aspect is dealt with thoroughly in each particular year. This was the approach chosen by Eumundi State School and it works well for them.

Following are the grades and the emphasis of their garden studies.

Prep:	Flowering Plants
Year 1:	Garden Vegetables
Year 2:	Beneficial Insects and Seed Gathering
Year 3:	Keeping Chooks
Year 4:	Water – Use and Conservation
Year 5:	Soils – Natural Ecosystems and Damaged Environments
Year 6:	Forests – Use and Conservation
Year 7:	Energy and Sustainable Housing

Their gardens are developing and the use by classes is increasing. Teachers have also found that incorporating the garden into the curriculum did reduce many of the problems they identified in the early planning workshops. So despite some staff changes, the gardens are continuing.

Their workload was reduced by developing planning templates, lesson plans and units of work very early in the process and sharing planning amongst teachers on the same grade. They also adopted the 12 Principles of Permaculture as expressed by David Holmgren and apply them to many aspects of their work across the curriculm.

Eumundi School has a strong Permaculture foundation, with a most capable permaculturist, Jon Gemmel, who has studied with Bill Mollison and Geoff Lawton, and is a leader in both the educational and practical aspects of the gardens.

They are also fortunate to have the support of one of the strongest permaculture groups in Australia, Permaculture Noosa, and many parents and teachers are members of the permaculture group.

It may seem as if a fortunate set of circumstances created the garden as a teaching resource, except that many schools, in completely different situations, are doing the same thing.

Eumundi school developed a whole school plan soon after they decided to add to their original eight year old permaculture garden that was out of sight from the classrooms and general playground areas, and to begin growing right outside the classrooms. It seems as if working in the garden under close supervision and within the usual learning program, allowed the children to become involved and to learn the basic skills in a short time. Even before the end of the first year, some children were asking to go back into the old garden and work to bring it back into full production.

This model does work well, but schools that have a number of composite classes or who have adopted a different curriculum model, may find this approach difficult. In some schools there is a greater risk that topics could be repeated or missed so they may require a topic or theme based program.

Approach 2
Units of Work

This was the way North Arm State School decided to proceed after a staff workshop on the garden and its uses identified it as a major educational resource and a way to improve the already exemplary learning experiences and outcomes for the children.

During a staff development day, teachers divided the school year into the four terms as columns and the year levels as rows. They filled in all the known topics/ themes/ units of work that they usually cover in a year. As the teachers volunteered their work units into the brainstorm, the work fell naturally across the four areas of;

1. Self and Others
2. Environment
3. Community
4. Creative Investigation

This created a new framework in which to place any new garden units. This step meant they were working from proven successes and not starting from scratch.

As the school motto is *"Lifelong Learning for Heart, Mind and Earth"* all units have an environmental or sustainability component and so support the school ethos.

This framework also clearly showed where there were gaps in working to the school vision. The staff decided that they would like to try to develop garden focused units to fill any gaps and to balance the learning aspects and vary the delivery.

As a staff they developed a school curriculum framework, the Island of Life model, which places major importance on teaching children all aspects of sustainability including good health. This has become a school focus, with the school garden at its core called, *"From Little Things Big Things Grow. From School to Community: Lifelong Learning for Healthy Futures".*

"It will provide core curriculum units of work that will fulfill our desire to have our students take control of one of the key determinants of their future health.

… a hierarchy of curriculum teaching units [will] be placed centrally in our school's curriculum framework. Outcomes from these units of work will be that children understand that eating well and high levels of physical activity are easy, and that natural activities go hand in hand to effect a healthy and happy life.

This curriculum renewal will benefit our community because it will provide the missing links, to integrate individual pockets of need and interest. It will provide our students their first real opportunity to see that they are themselves powerful instruments in determining their own future health and well being.

Support for our school's curriculum focus on sustainability, is abundant. North Arm is a very strong community. The staff, parent and wider community are jointly and strongly committed to children's health and well being. We teach health and sustainability because our children are in the demographic whose health and lifestyle predictions are dire. In time chronic ill health will overtake many of them if they do not find the resources within themselves to swim against the tide of poor nutrition and inactivity. This curriculum will point them in the right direction to find those resources."

North Arm Planning Document December, 2007

A few of the units suggested for them or to stimulate planning ideas are reproduced at the end of this chapter. The units have been taken up and changed, as hoped, by teachers managing the needs of their learners, the resources available and the curriculum demands. Each time a teacher uses one of the units the form and content will be very different from another teacher's use and delivery. Units will continue to vary even with the same teacher working with a different group especially in ever evolving gardens.

North Arm school garden is about to be re-developed and additional growing spaces, close to classrooms and walkways, are being established.

The school works closely with parents and community groups, so the new gardens are becoming a focal point for school and community interaction.

But even beyond the *"From Little Things Big Things Grow"* sustainability curriculum emphasis, classes are incorporating the school gardens into all of the Key Learning Areas to ensure that the lessons of the classroom are anchored in the real world. Through the school garden they are ensuring that the children have every opportunity to participate in meaningful learning activities where they can reinforce the class work and demonstrate their abilities across all learning areas.

Teachers at North Arm referred to the prepared units as models and took into account the Elemental Learnings for Sustainability presented in the following approach.

Approach 3

This approach involves looking at all the skills and knowledge required to be able to grow a garden as well as to understand all the basic sustainability issues. It is a basic bag of skills and knowledge that is the birthright of every child in our society to ensure their ability to provide for themselves and to work with nature to ensure health for themselves and the planet.

It was compiled by referencing the 'Permaculture Designers' Manual' by Bill Mollison and adding aspects of the work of David Holmgren in 'Permaculture, Beyond Sustainability' and so has both strong practical elements as well as sound application of principles to the challenges we are now facing and will face well into the future of this and subsequent generations.

There was a degree of difficulty in adapting the theory and the practice to the primary school level as both texts are aimed at adult readers and the concepts can be difficult to grasp even for grown ups. If presented experientially and in logical sequence over time, children grasp these concepts easily and incorporate them into 'common sense'.

The Elementals

Teachers are always asking what the skills and knowledge sets are for learning and working in gardens and towards understanding sustainability. Knowing where to start and how to guide children through learning experiences appropriate for their stage of development and prior experiences, is a way to begin whole school planning for outdoor adventures and learning.

Presented here are lists that attempt to cover the foundation knowledge for work in the school garden and which then expand to address the full range of sustainability issues. The lists are by no means complete or refined and are offered here as a guideline for teachers when planning. Teaches can pick and choose, adapt or write their own to use as a valuable tool in future planning processes.

The name of 'Elementals' was selected as they are truly the most elementary of all skills and knowledge needed for basic self reliance and the understanding of natural systems and their drivers. Once known, these elementals can form the thinking in subject areas that are far from the garden but still based on systems thinking that is so easily learned when playing, learning and growing outdoors.

So the elementals form a collection of elementary understandings in science which are learned in the school garden and then form the building blocks for thinking, learning and acting in the real world.

These elementary learnings have been divided into topics that may stand alone but are usually clustered together in themed work, projects or as part of rich tasks.

The topics are:

1. Climate
2. Patterns in Nature
3. Water
4. Earth Resources
5. Landform
6. Living Soil
7. Plants
8. Animals
9. Trees
10. Energy
11. Buildings and Structures
12. Permaculture Design

The list under each heading is divided into Lower, Middle and Upper Primary school and some of this work could be extended appropriately up to Year 10. There is a logical sequence to the Elementals that builds on previous work, so if a group has not worked on the early skills, then start where they are and move quickly to their appropriate level.

The first topic, Climate has the blank space ready for teachers to list all the things they already do to support the suggested learnings – some may only need a tick. Doing this exercise will identify those things not covered. Then, with another colour, teachers can add the activities, exercises or units of work that will support each unaddressed learning. For the sake of space, and ease of copying, we have not reproduced the blank space for the rest. If teachers wish to do the exercise, then they can copy the Elemental lists and glue them onto the left hand side of a blank sheet ready to complete.

When completing the sheets, it will become noticeable that some elementals are well covered by programmed theme or unit work for the grade, while others are not. It is also likely that the knowledge components are better covered than the skill aspects. Without real hands-on work and actually watching the children perform the task on a number of occasions in different contexts, skills are not truly assessable. So without a school garden accessing garden skills is very difficult.

Climate

Outdoor Studies	Covered by Cross Curricula Study
Lower Primary **Skills** Observing the weather. Recording simple weather details. Reading a compass to locate North, South, East and West. Reading a wind vane. Noting and celebrating the passing of the seasons. Watching the path of the sun. **Knowledge** Different cloud forms and how that can predict some weather. Wind effects and wind direction. Understanding condensation and evaporation. Humidity.	
Middle Primary **Skills** Measuring weather details using instruments and relating them to growing seasons and plant species selection. Examining the differences/ similarities between the local and a different climatic zone. **Knowledge** Influence on climate of latitude, altitude and position in relation to oceans and continents. The major climatic regions of the globe. Reasons for the seasonal changes. Causes of droughts and floods.	
Upper Primary **Skills** Measuring and reporting weather details. Communicating with people in other climatic regions regarding the effects on their food production, way of life and the weather disasters they prepare for. Performing a Sector Analysis for a specified site. (See Permaculture Elementals) Designing a home for people, or an animal shelter that takes into account the climatic effects of a specified/ selected region. **Knowledge** Sector planning. Map reading (contours, flood levels). Global weather patterns and what drives them.	

Patterns in Nature

Outdoor Studies

Lower Primary

Skills

Observing patterns in nature.
Making collections of natural things
and putting these things into categories
of the student's choosing.

Knowledge

The natural world is made up of
natural shapes and patterns.
Patterns in nature are repeated.
The same patterns are found throughout
the natural world. (Many things in nature
look like other things in nature.)
Patterns in nature perform functions.

Middle Primary

Skills

Naming common natural patterns.
Finding a certain pattern in many different places
and in different scales (or orders of pattern).
e.g.; branching in leaves, trees,
vascular systems and rivers.
Listing the patterns seen in the
school garden and grounds.

Knowledge

There are mathematical patterns evident
in nature.
One of these patterns is the Fibonacci Series.
Vocabulary.
Recognise branching, dendritic, spiral, sphere.

Upper Primary

Skills

Linking a pattern and a function in the
school gardens or the bioregion.

Knowledge

Some patterns are moving and occur
in moving air or water (The Ekman
Spiral and the Von Karman Trail).
Fractals are visible in nature and can be created
by repeating a mathematical formula.

Water

Outdoor Studies

Lower Primary

Skills

Pouring, watering gardens; using
a watering can, or hose.

Knowledge

Water is a liquid but can be a gas or a solid.
Water runs down hill.
Water is essential for life of plants and animals.
We need to drink more water in hot weather.
How to catch water.
The duties and uses of water.

Middle Primary

Skills

Pouring accurately.
Measuring in millilitres, litres and mega litres.
Adjusting water flows.
Watering gardens.
Selecting watering schedules for optimum
growth and minimum water loss.

Knowledge

The Water Cycle.
Creeks and Rivers (orders of streams).
Moving water carries materials, (soil in erosion).
Moving water as an energy source.
Water can dissolve nutrients and pollutants.
How to catch and store water.
Finding water in the bush or desert.

Upper Primary

Skills

Catching, storing and moving water.
Designing simple watering systems.
Reading a simple contour map.
Marking contours.
Conducting a water audit.

Knowledge

The duties of water.
Measuring water volumes.
Water pressure and how it is achieved (height of
storage, size of conduit, and distance from source).
Water travels at close to 90 degrees to contour.
Strategies to slow and stop water flows.
Cleaning water and grey water systems.
Dendritic pattern.
Water in our bioregion (natural systems, dams,
etc; individual home and property strategies).

Earth Resources	Landform

Outdoor Studies

Lower Primary

Skills

Identifying and manipulating soils and rocks.
Making items from earth resources.

Knowledge

The Earth provides all the resources used
by man.
People have used earth resources for
many thousands of years.
Our Earth's history is stored in rock strata.
Vocabulary;
clay, ochres, salt, precious stones
and metals, fossils, fossil fuels.

Middle Primary

Skills

Creating useful items from clay and
firing them.
Identifying common rocks in the region.
Making ochres from soil and using
them in paints and/ or renders.

Knowledge

Minerals in the earth and mining.
Common uses of local minerals.
The soil strata locally or in the school
grounds (observing a soil core reading to
identify topsoil, subsoil parent rock).

Upper Primary

Skills

Building in mud brick or clay cob
(model or community project).
Designing and creating a useful or aesthetic item
from earth resources extracted by
the designer.

Knowledge

Building materials used in areas of study (depends
on or influenced by other subject area planning).
Earth resources in our bioregion.

Outdoor Studies

Lower Primary

Skills

Playing in sand pit.
Building in soil pit and adding water.
Finding the resting angle of wet and
dry sand, clay, silt and rocks.
Observing flat land and hills in
our community.

Knowledge

Vocabulary;
river flats, hill, ridge, mountain, river, creek, gully.

Middle Primary

Skills

Identifying common rocks in the region.

Knowledge

How the local land was formed
(water, wind, uplifts etc).
The soil strata locally or in the school
grounds (observing a soil core reading to
identify topsoil, subsoil parent rock).

Upper Primary

Skills

Locating the key point of a hill.
Observing and selecting the best sites for water
catchments and storages in the landscape.
Selecting a good site for a garden.

Knowledge

Various landforms across the globe; deserts,
mountain rages, volcanoes, wetlands,
forests, heath, tundra or river systems.
What determines our bioregion – the
rivers, hills and mountains.
The terminology for all landforms in our bioregion.

Living Soil

Outdoor Studies

Lower Primary

Skills

Using hand tools to dig in sand and soil.
Digging holes in preparation for planting
  (seed, cuttings, seedlings and plants).
Recognising different components of a
  garden soil (sand, compost, loam).
Feeding worms in a worm farm.
Adding to a compost heap.

Knowledge

Life cycle of a worm.
Beneficial activities of the worm.
Compost turns to humus.
Humus is formed by nature in forests
  and other natural systems.

Middle Primary

Skills

Creating a healthy soil.
Building a No-Dig Garden.
Testing the pH of soils.

Knowledge

The pH needs of plants in the school garden.
The process of decay.
Bacteria.
Fungi.

Upper Primary

Skills

Making humus from compost (building
  a compost heap monitoring temperature
  and the decomposition process).
Moving soil with spades, shovels and rakes.
Preparing soil for planting trees and shrubs.
Observing soil life with a microscope.

Knowledge

How to manipulate soil pH to suit
  particular plant species.
Identification of common soil biota.
Soils in our bioregion;
    earth resources, farming soils, wetlands,
    degraded soils and forest floor.

Plants

Outdoor Studies

Lower Primary

Skills

Collecting seed for observation and identification.
Sprouting seeds.
Growing plants from seeds.
Identify some edible plants in the
  school vegetable garden.
Preparing some edible plants for eating.

Knowledge

Seeds come in many different shapes and sizes.
Seeds have mechanisms for dispersal.
Plants are living things.
Plants require sunlight, water and
  nutrients from the soil to grow.
Some plants are edible.
Not all plants have seeds for reproduction.

Middle Primary

Skills

Propagating plants from collected
  seed and cuttings.
Saving seeds.
Recognising a healthy and a sick plant.
Identification of 10 edible plants in the
  school grounds or the locality.

Knowledge

Parts of a plant.
The life cycle of a flowering and
  a non flowering plant.
Weeds as indicators of soil condition.
Weeds as repairers of damaged soils.

Upper Primary

Skills

Propagating and grafting useful plants.
Selecting appropriate plant species for the
  vegetable garden, orchard or flower garden.
Successfully planting at least five edible plants
  and monitoring their health for several weeks.
Identifying five native plants.

Knowledge

Visiting and observing a local
  productive plant system.
Visiting and observing a local natural plant system.
How to establish a plant system
  in the school or at home.

Animals

Outdoor Studies

Lower Primary

Skills

Meeting some of the needs of an animal
(worms, fish, frogs, chickens, guinea pigs
or larger animals) for several weeks.

Knowledge

Animals are living things that have general needs
and some specific needs for each species.
General characteristics of animal classes.
Animals can have several uses in a garden.

Middle Primary

Skills

Meeting all the needs of an animal
over several weeks.
Following the life cycle of an animal in the
school garden (butterflies, frogs, lizards).
Identifying animals, birds and insects
that use the school garden.
Providing shelter for animals in the school
garden. (diurnal and nocturnal)
Placing and observing bird boxes,
rocks, small ponds etc.
Making use of an animal product
(manure, eggs, feathers etc).

Knowledge

Animals reproduce in different ways.
Animal shelter and homes.
Animals have been useful to man
throughout history.
Animal farms produce animals to
meet many human needs.

Upper Primary

Skills

Designing an animal shelter that meets all
the needs of the selected animal species.
Listing the needs of a farmed animal species.
Recognising a healthy or sick animal.
Using the products of an animal in a school
garden system* so that there is no waste.

Knowledge

The functioning of an animal system in the
bioregion, through visiting a working farm.

*Moral issue of the humane treatment of animals.

Trees

Outdoor Studies

Lower Primary

Skills

Identifying a tree from other plants.
Observing some functions of trees (shade, shelter,
habitat, erosion control, fruit, timber etc).

Knowledge

Characteristics of a tree.
Parts of a tree.
Forests more than just groups of trees.
The composition of a forest floor.

Middle Primary

Skills

Planting a tree.
Identifying 10 trees in the school
gardens or local community.
Identify a healthy and a sick tree.
Identify five native and five exotic trees.

Knowledge

Mulch as a replacement for the forest leaf litter.
Food forests as designed systems.
Different trees perform different functions
in a natural or designed system.
The uses of three native and
three exotic tree species.

Upper Primary

Skills

Planting or maintaining a tree system
(conservation or food production).
Identify 10 native species.
Identify 10 food tree species.
Identify five support species (those trees that help
the establishment and growth of a target tree).

Knowledge

Tree systems in the local bioregion.
Using trees to modify climate.
Using trees to produce food.
Trees and forests as modifiers of global climate.
The uses of trees in permaculture design.
Community organisations that support
tree planting eg; Landcare.

Energy

Outdoor Studies

Lower Primary

Skills

Making things move by using moving water and moving air
 (Paddlewheels, sailing boats etc).

Growing plants using the energy from the sun.

Knowledge

Energy, in the form of food, is needed to keep plants and animals alive and for them to grow.

Energy is the ability to do work or the ability to move and change things.

Without energy nothing happens.

Energy is required to make machines and technologies work.

Energy from the sun is stored in fossil fuels such as oil, coal and gas.

Turning lights and fans off when not in use saves energy.

Appliances in your home have energy ratings.

Middle Primary

Skills

Observing and reporting on the harnessing of a form of energy
 used to power a specified tool, machine or device.

Listing energy sources used in the school.

Reporting on the energy transmitters in the local region.

Calculating the energy use of your school and how it may be reduced.

Reading and making graphs of the home or school energy use.

Knowledge

Basic understanding of the process of photosynthesis.

The Power Grid and the energy source used to power it.

Energy sources; solar, wind, hydro, tidal, geothermal.

Energy transmitters; electricity, steam, compressed air.

Timeline of energy source discoveries and use e.g.;

- ✸ Wood was the first fuel used by man.
- ✸ Coal replaced wood as supplies diminished.
- ✸ The first oil well was drilled in 1859.
- ✸ Travel uses energy. Goods that travel add 'travel miles' to their production energy.

The energy used in production is called 'embodied energy' and is called the eMergy of an item.

Heating and cooling require energy. Good design and planting can reduce energy needs of buildings.

Upper Primary

Skills

Using an alternative energy source to perform a function most often
 performed by electricity from the grid or a fossil fuel.

Listing energy sources used in the local region.

Reporting on the energy transmitters in the local region.

Rating energy efficiency.

Using equipment to calculate energy and energy efficiency (thermometer, light meters, etc).

Knowledge

The combustion engine.

Appropriate energy source for specific functions.

Harnessing energy to perform work.

The earth is a closed system.

Living things are open systems and rely on energy flows.

Simple passive solar principles for building design.

Thermal mass and how it can modify temperature changes.

The solar chimney.

Buildings and Structures

Outdoor Studies

Lower Primary

Skills

Identifying buildings and their
purposes in our community.
Identifying common building
materials in our community.
Listing the fencing styles and
materials in our community.

Knowledge

Buildings are designed to fulfil a function.
Local building materials are often
used in local constructions.
Buildings are warmed and cooled
by many different methods.
Hot air rises and cool air sinks.
Condensation warms and evaporation cools.
Fences have several uses.

Middle Primary

Skills

Matching a construction to a climatic zone.
Recognising the specific purpose of a construction.
Reading a simple building plan.
Drawing the scale drawing of the classroom.
Building a model of a simple building.
Categorising buildings according to use.
Measuring the length of fences.
Preparing a materials list to build a specified fence.

Knowledge

People in different parts of the world design
their homes and buildings to best suit the
materials they have and their climate.
Scale drawing techniques.
Measuring length and area.
Cultural differences in the way people build fences.

Upper Primary

Skills

Designing a building to perform a specific
function (home, workspace, animal shelter).
Considering methods of warming
and cooling a building.
Considering ways of providing water to a building.
Building a simple fence (for animals or trellising).

Knowledge

How to orient a building to take
advantage of passive solar effects.
Thermal mass.
Multiple functions of fences.
Simple fence construction techniques.

Permaculture

Outdoor Studies

Lower Primary

Skills

Identifying some of the characteristics of a
permaculture garden; mixed species planting,
mulched beds, curved paths, water storages,
companion planting, multifunction,
perennials etc.

Knowledge

Permaculture is a way of providing the needs
of people with less environmental damage.
Permaculture has three ethics;
Care of Earth and species,
Care of People and Fair Share.
Permaculture techniques provide
clean and healthy food.

Middle Primary

Skills

Selecting a garden site.
Growing food in a permaculture garden.
Contributing to recycling materials
within the school.

Knowledge

Understanding the need for Sector Planning.
Understanding the need for Zonal Planning.
Observing the Edge Effect.
Permaculture is based on two sets
of principles that tell us;
1. How to behave as responsible producers.
2. How to produce and meet our needs.

Upper Primary

Skills

Making a simple zonal plan of the
classroom or school garden.
Doing a simple sector plan for the garden or a
building taking into account light, heat and wind.
Recycling materials within the school.
Gaining a yield from a permaculture garden.
Harvesting and preparing a permaculture product.
Participating in a community market.

Knowledge

Communities need to share resources.
When to harvest specified produce
from the permaculture garden.
Local trading systems.

Using the Elementals as a Tool

It is assessment and reporting initiatives from education departments that require children to actually do things or perform tasks to demonstrate (deep) understanding. Testing knowledge is straightforward, questions can be asked, tests administered. But to show understanding it is necessary for a child to use that knowledge and apply it in a real situation, a number of times and in various contexts to show that the learning in one situation has transferred to another.

This assessment and reporting is very much like the competency-based education in the Vocational Education Sector, where candidates for assessment either can or cannot perform a task (yet).

School gardens offer a huge range of opportunities to demonstrate knowledge, skills or abilities that are difficult to measure in the intensely supervised confines of a classroom. These opportunities range from teamwork, occupational health and safety issues, the ability to follow instructions, to the practical skills of growing, harvesting and preparing food and inter-personal relationships.

Once a teacher has selected the topics, copied the pages, cut off those levels that do not pertain to their current group, they can fill in the blank sides with the work they already do.

There will be some Elementals not covered in any other way, so bundle them into units of work. To help with the school year program planning, they can be cut and laid onto a blank sheet where they can be moved around into logical groups. Each group should have a knowledge set and a skill set. The skill set is the one that will suggest what the children will need to do. And the knowledge set will be the things they need to know to do the activity.

By looking at the skills, a teacher can plan an outdoor activity such as building a garden, working with chickens, making compost or harvesting and selling produce from the garden that will incorporate all the elementals not yet covered. And by looking at the associated knowledge the teacher will be able to see all the lessons or the instruction that needs to be given to the children.

Now label your rough draft sheet with the broad unit titles. (There are model units prepared at the end of this chapter with some suggested unit headings.) Any Elementals that don't fit under one title, can be moved to incorporate into another unit.

Your rough draft sheet may have identified the need for practical garden work, understanding another climatic region, identifying edible plants, so in this situation you would be looking for a food garden topic. So we can use 'Making a Pizza Garden' as an example. This one is completed for you so you can get an idea of the usefulness of the template and you can make the necessary changes.

Using the Template as a Planning Tool

It is very easy to work straight onto the blank template so make a copy to work on.

Start with the Overview and brainstorm all the things you think you could do. Some will come now and others you can go back and fill in once prompted by the various headings as you work through the template.

Include other subject areas that may need to have some excitement injected into them. This could be mathematics, reading or writing or indeed any subject that needs some connection to the real world or nature. This should always be as natural as possible. Highly contrived units can become tiresome and children can lose interest if everything they do in a day is about pizzas or gardens. But you could expect to include some of the following depending on the duration of the unit:

- finding or writing a pizza recipe
- researching the foods used in a pizza
- reporting on the origin of the pizza
- locating the geographic origin of pizzas
- describing a Mediterranean climate
- customs, food and clothing in Mediterranean countries
- a visitor from Italy. Interviews and reports
- creative writing such as 'The Pizza that Refused to be Eaten'
- songs, poems and art from Italy

- researching major Italian cities
- posters on healthy home made pizzas
- dough making
- why are pizzas circular?
- measuring diameters of the standard small, medium and large pizzas
- measuring the weight of the standard pizza
- deciding the best value pizza
- costing the homemade pizza and comparing it with the store bought ones
- graphing pizza topping favourites across the grade

The list can go on as the potential is huge and depends on what is happening in the classroom, the garden and the community as well as the learning needs of the children.

If the children can suggest things they would like to know or be able to do, then the likelihood of having higher interest levels and engagement increases significantly. Let them ask the questions and suggest some activities.

Once you have collected your thoughts, ideas and the input from the learners, then use the Unit Planner Template to build the unit. (See the examples on the following pages.)

1. Label the Unit and state the grade level, the anticipated duration of the work and which areas of the school grounds you will utilise.

2. Write a brief overview of what you think you might do and present and make a list of questions or things to be explored as a result of your brainstorm.

3. Look through the *Elementals* at your grade level and select the ones that fit with your overview. (Or copy the ones you have already identified from your rough draft planning sheet.)

4. Add in the *basic skills* and concepts which can be made authentic and relevant by having this unit as a focus.

5. List the *values* you wish to promote and the *behaviours* that you hope to form through work in this unit.

6. Put in any areas for *special treatment*. These could be basic skills or mathematical operations that have become a bit tedious through reliance on worksheets and text books. They may be attitudes or values around issues such as bullying or racism. Practicing teachers will be very aware of these special areas as they are a regular feature of addressing the learning needs of any group.

7. List the *processes* that will be emphasised. This gives teachers the opportunity to address processes that may not be treated in other ways and to ensure there is a variety of processes that will keep student interest high and provide a diversity of activities.

8. List as many new terms as you can and add the ones that will crop up during the unit. This *vocabulary* development can be incorporated into both spelling and written expression lessons.

9. Address the assessment of all the curriculum links 1-8 (Elementals, Basic Skills, Values and Behaviours, Vocabulary, Area for Special Treatment and Processes to be Emphasised). Then list the *assessment tools*. These may be simply the evidence from the activities or you may choose to create quizzes, find-a-words and matching activities that demonstrate understanding.

10. *Reporting* will involve the way the outcomes from work in the unit is communicated to the child, the parent and subsequent teachers. List the vehicles for reporting which may be checklists, statements, photographic records, presentations, report cards or any other options for reporting.

11. *Evaluation* by the teacher is critical to the improvement of the unit over time and to the development of the garden and its links back to the classroom. So this section should be completed at the end of a unit. In the model some typical comments are shown to give you an idea just how helpful this section can be.

Assessment and Reporting

If you have trouble with Point 9 above, then on your rough draft, make a list of all the skills, knowledge, behaviours and values that could be learned and demonstrated through work in this unit. (In our example; 'Making a Pizza Garden'.)

Build the list by referencing

1. **The Elementals.**
2. **Basic skills** appropriate to the grade level.
3. **Values and Behaviours** that are required by government or school policies.
4. **Areas for Special Treatment.** This would be any particular skill, knowledge, value or behaviour that has been difficult to treat or assess in any other way.
5. **Processes to be Emphasized.** Units will vary in the processes used in its study. Teachers can balance the thinking, learning and expression processes by placing varying emphasis within the different units.

For example, team work is difficult to assess in a variety of contexts without taking the learning outdoors. Some children who find indoor group work, that relies quite heavily on academic ability, a struggle. But in practical activities away from the triggers of low self-esteem, those same children can excel in group work outside (and vice versa).

Health and safety issues are also more critical when working in the outdoors. And there are many others that have been discussed in the earlier chapters that make assessment of outdoor learning so very important.

It is only when you have identified what the children should know and should be able to do, that you can plan how this knowledge and these abilities can be assessed.

List the activities and the lessons. Some of the lessons will be taking in new information and some will be activities. Some of the doing can actually be part of the assessment so you can use check lists to tick off the relevant skills and knowledge.

Where checklists are not adequate and evidence is required then the lists, reports, work journals, completed activity sheets, quizzes and so on will show competency.

This unit model has been completed for a particular group. Your group, resources and constraints will be different and it is offered here as a demonstration of the template and the potential for learning in the garden.

Suggestions for Units

Some units have been planned to give you an idea of the sort of information to be recorded under the specific headings.

The headings are designed to be generic so that teachers in all states can adapt them to their own current departmental guidelines. Any of the Unit Title suggestions can be adapted for any grade and so will be very different because of the different Elementals and curriculum demands.

Nothing is prescriptive and meant only to give teachers an idea of the potential of integrating the outdoors into the curriculum

Unit	Title	Grade Level	Duration in weeks
1.	Growing a Pizza Garden	Upper	8
2.	LUNCH IN A BOX	MIDDLE	6 -12
3.	AFTER A RAIN EVENT	MIDDLE	2
4.	SEEDS	LOWER	4 - 8
5.	PATTERNS IN NATURE THE Fibonacci Series	UPPER	2

The native Australian snail displays the spiral pattern of the Fibonacci Series.

Title: Growing a Pizza Garden	Grade: Upper Primary	Duration: 8 weeks	Outdoor areas utilised: Section of vegetable garden, cob oven, green house, pots outside classroom

Overview

Listing the vegetables used in a pizza.
Listing all ingredients and how they may be accessed. Costing a pizza that is bought, one that is ready made, one that is home made and one that has some home-grown ingredients.
Finding the origin of these vegetables and identifying the climatic zone/s they come from.
Describing the best growing conditions for the vegetables.
Preparing a garden bed. Planting the vegetables appropriately. Caring for the plants during growth.
Harvesting the vegetables.
Preparing a pizza.
Using a cob/ pizza oven.
Celebration of Italian culture and its contribution to our Australian way of life.

Scope of Curriculum Links

1. Elementals

Climate
Communicating with people in other climatic regions regarding the effects on their food production, way of life and the weather disasters they prepare for.
The Mediterranean Climate, and the plants that grow well in those conditions.

Permaculture
Locating the best position and time to grow a pizza garden.
(Well drained, sunny spot, low humidity).
Gaining a yield from the garden.
Harvesting and preparing a product (the pizza).
When to harvest

Trees
Identify the olive tree.

Living soil.
Moving soil.
Preparing soil for planting.
Measuring and altering the soil pH.

Plants
Species selection.
Planting five different species.
Monitoring plant health.

2. Basic skills and concepts appropriate to the grade level

Mathematics
Properties of the circle. Graphing pizza topping preferences (bar and pie graphs). Budgeting.
Costing commercial pizza and comparing with the home made variety. Graphing comparisons.

Written Expression
Recipes, advertising the pizza day/ product, report on the olive tree.

Geography
Italy. Major Italian cities.
Climate and landform of Italy.
Writing to schools in Italy (email).

Cultural Studies
Italian lifestyle, food, clothes, special days, invitation to Italian visitor to the class.
Italian immigration to Australia and the cultural benefits.

Art
Famous artists, sculptors and painters of Italy.

Reading/ Research
The Italian sense of style in fashion, car design, furniture etc.

3. Values and behaviours
Appreciation of the diversity of cultures in Australia. Valuing diversity.
Sense of personal achievement when producing food from the garden to the table.
Good healthy eating. Social importance of food and eating. Valuing cultural heritage.

4. Area for special treatment
Making the mathematics lessons more related to the real world. Incorporating a lot of calculations for the garden set up, the planting, the costing and the amount of product to show the relevance of learning mathematical operations and getting them correct.

5. Processes to be emphasised
Planning, observing, predicting, sharing.

Vocabulary

Pizza, Italy, Italian, Mediterranean, circular, segment, sector, diameter, radius, dough, toppings, choice, sauce, capsicum, tomato, onion, garlic, cheese, eggplant, mushrooms, Mozzarella, soft, crunchy, crisp, thick, thin, (and the superlatives; thicker, thickest) oven, cob, bake, roast, knead, share, fraction, half, quarter.

Assessment Tools to be Used

1. Elementals
Garden establishment.
Garden journal completion.
Design of garden, lists of materials required, costings of the garden, watering schemes,
 pH levels and how it could be/ was improved, species lists, harvesting the produce.
Worksheets.
Preparing the pizzas and watching/ timing the use of the pizza oven under supervision.

2. Basic skills
Production of accurate graphs.
Report on olive trees.
Identifying five Italian cities on the map and linking them with famous landmarks, people, inventions.
Pizza Day celebration, cooking the pizzas, costume, art works, delivery of the material to one or more other groups.
Italian music, song and dance.
Learning some Italian words and phrases.

3. Values and behaviours
Pizza Day celebration, the flavour and quality of the vegetables and the pizzas produced.
Garden work journals.
Relationship with students of Italian descent.

4. Area for special treatment
Raised interest level in mathematics.
Increased accuracy in calculations.
Transfer of the skills and attitude to other areas of mathematics and the other subject areas.

List of Evidence to Gather

Photographs, emails to schools in Italy, a recipe, graphs, garden work
 journal, report on olive trees, posters, Italian cities' quiz.

Reporting and Evaluation

Photographs and video made to be shown to parents or put into foyer display for parents to see.
Students to self-assess and report on the success of their garden,
 the pizza they prepared and the success of the celebration day.
Teacher to make anecdotal remarks regarding the behaviours and values of targeted students during this unit.
 (Those who have shown some sort of cultural bias against others from a Mediterranean ethnic background,
 those who have not accepted the relevance of mathematics in their daily life etc.)

Evaluation (after the event may include the following considerations)
Garden site well suited.
Vegetables took longer to ripen than expected.
Good support from members of the Italian community, need larger plot next time.
Library resources need to include more references on Italian art.

Title: Lunch in a Box/Pot	Grade: Middle Primary	Duration: 6-12 weeks	Outdoor areas utilised: Window ledges, verandas, space close to classroom or potting shed, seed garden

Overview

Healthy eating. Discussion of fresh food. Value of locally grown and organic food.
Researching and selecting salad and/ or stir-fry vegetable varieties to grow in a polystyrene box, pots or large pot.
Deciding on a species selection process (survey, personal choices, graphing survey results).
Researching requirements for the species selected. Preparing the planting containers.
Seed collection from the plants in seed garden or from the school seed bank.
Choose seeds or seedlings (for the appropriate level). Seed raising to seedling size.
Planting the salad vegetables/ stir-fry vegetables. Observing the growth and responding to the needs of the growing plants.
Making measurements of the growth (at the appropriate level).
Comparing growth in different varieties, conditions and positions.
Recording measurements and comparisons at the appropriate level in mathematics and vocabulary development.
Researching recipes for salads and dressings. Recording recipes for stir-fry vegetables.
Harvesting and eating the salads and/ or the vegetables.
Covering one or more containers with plastic or create terrarium to see/ compare effect on growing.
Study the water cycle to appropriate level.
Cultural studies relating to cultures using salads and/ or cultures that stir-fry.
Visitors from those cultures for presentations and demonstrations to the class.

Scope of Curriculum Links

1. Elementals

Climate

Using weather details collected to decide on the best time and best species to plant to obtain a lunch in a box/ pot. (Revision of seasonal knowledge.)
Relating climatic information to the cultural aspect of stir-fry vegetables (Asian Greens).
Researching the latitude and longitude of the salad or vegetable varieties and their use in traditional cooking.

Water

Watering gardens. Water dissolves nutrients for the plant to take up.
Catching and storing water for use in growing a salad or stir-fry.

Landform

Mimicking the drainage systems in nature to create drainage in the box/ pot.

Permaculture

Sector analysis to find the best site for the boxes/ pots. Zone 1 is close to the home.
How to become a responsible producer. How to produce and meet our own needs.

Living soil

Creating a healthy soil. Testing the pH of the soil.

Plants

Propagating from collected seeds. Recognising a sick or healthy plant. Identification of 10 edible plants.

2. Basic skills and concepts appropriate to the grade level

Mathematics

Graphing food preferences. Expressing as a ratio or fraction.
Calculating volume of soil mix required for the box or the pot. Calculating/ measuring the volume of water used to produce the crop. Practical applications for the four basic operations and problem solving. Creating a budget for the project - costing resources required, measuring and valuing the produce. Developing a time line (days and months).

Science

Parts of a plant. Plant reproduction. Plant growth. Insects that may visit the boxes or pots. Identifying useful or harmful insects in the garden. Sun and temperature effects on plant growth. Research the geographical origin of some of the plants selected. herbivores, omnivores and carnivores. The water cycle (terrarium activity).

Cultural Studies

Selecting a culture that utilises the species selected and research the food, clothing, language and customs of that culture. Discuss the influence that culture has on our own.

Writing

Experience in the following genres: lists, reports, recipes, instructions, schedules, poster (healthy lunches) as well as some creative writing and poetry.

Reading

Timetables, planting guides and instructions, recipes and research.

Health

Healthy eating, human nutrition, food requirements for humans. Diet types (vegetarian, vegan)

3. Values and behaviours

Good planning results in gaining the desired outcome. Consistent good results occur as a consequence of good thinking and planning. Research leads to better planning. Graphs can give us a clear picture of data collected. When gardening, you can learn a lot from making a mistake. There are benefits to self-reliance or being a producer not just a consumer. Fresh organic food is good for optimum human health.

4. Area for special treatment	5. Processes to be emphasised
Teachers may select any area that links to this topic where interest, engagement, or authenticity is not working as well as it should. Potential areas of revitalisation and motivation that may be most specific to this unit would be; Mathematics, Cultural Studies and Science.	surveying, graphing, researching, calculating, recording, reporting, planting, harvesting, preparing. (Teachers can emphasise any process that is not well covered in other curriculum areas.)

Understandings

Planning will result in a better product. All experiences are a learning opportunity. You can provide for yourself with the right skills, knowledge and resources. Eating fresh food can help achieve good health. The amount of water in the Earth's atmosphere is static but it changes form and place. Nutrients in the soil we grow in are taken up by plants and then ingested by animals and humans. We can only be as healthy as our soils. Microcosms can show the same global processes as the macrocosm and these processes occur all over the globe.

Vocabulary

Planting, propagation, heritage varieties, seed bank, aspect, drainage, selection, pest management, seed raising mixture, soil testing.

Assessment Tools to be Used

1. Elementals	2. Basic skills
Make a survey and record information pictorially or graphically. Research appropriate plant varieties for salad and how they may be presented in a salad. Establish, maintain, harvest and prepare salad vegetables. (record in a journal or as a checklist). Create a poster or presentation that shows an understanding of the basics of human nutrition and healthy eating Growing a salad/ stir-fry vegetables and preparation of a salad.	Solving simple mathematical problems related to the establishment, maintenance and harvest of salad or stir-fry vegetables. (The four basic operations, some measurement of length, volume and weight.) Make lists of selected species, tasks or resources required. Fill in the blanks of a water cycle diagram Comprehension exercises and cloze passages based on the garden work. Adhering to a budget.
3. Values and behaviours Teacher checklists, journal records, observation of behavioural changes. Changes/ improvement in work-attitude, understanding or motivation.	4. Area for special treatment **Cultural Studies** Change in attitude to members of other ethnic groups. Willingness to try something from another culture. **Mathematics** Increased interest, engagement and accuracy. Teachers can design an activity with a product that will demonstrate work in the area for special treatment they selected. This will then be their assessment tool.

List of Evidence to Gather

Teachers will create this list from the activities they have designed in this unit and they should cover a variety of tools. Activities should be varied with written (reports, completed work-sheets), drawn (posters and illustrated records), spoken (oral reports, presentations) and actions (demonstrations, working groups).

Reporting and Evaluation

Reporting on this unit would be done best by recording and sharing the growing and harvesting of the produce. This may be done by inviting parents and the principal to the lunch from the box or showing the video or photos to parents.
Comments in the journal will inform parents and subsequent teachers as to work ethic and behaviours.
Other results can be reported as for other topics that demonstrate skills and knowledge in the Key Learning Areas.

Evaluation

This will depend on what worked and didn't work during the unit, the potential for further links and comments about how the unit worked to engage the students' interest in the Key Learning Areas. This should be used by the teacher when planning this unit in the future and to inform other teachers who may also want to use the unit with their class.

Title: After a Rain Event	Grade: Middle Primary	Duration: 2 weeks	Outdoor areas utilised: Vegetable garden, bushland
Overview		This unit is designed to be easily adapted for lower or upper primary grades.	

Observation of an outdoor area after rain. This may be a garden, an area of playground or bushland.
Children may generate or be given a list of questions.
They should have the opportunity to make their own observations and propose new questions in the field.
Students can record in words, drawings or in photos the answers to the questions.
Students are encouraged to devise their own method of reporting one or more of their observations.
Some model questions are;

- How much rain fell during the rain event? Over what period was the event?
- Was the rain typical or unusual for the time of the year? How does it compare to rainfall in other years?
- Have any garden materials moved during the rain? Which ones and how far did they travel?
- Can you show the direction of the water flow? How did it enter and leave the garden area?
- What were the beneficial effects of the rain?
- What are any of the negative effects of the rain?
- Has the rain caused any damage to plants? Which ones?
- How could any of the damage be minimised?
- How have any creatures in the garden responded to the rain event and its aftermath?
- Can we make better use of the rain that falls on our school grounds?
- Was the water clean when it left our school grounds?

Scope of Curriculum Links

1. Elementals

Climate
Measuring weather details using instruments. Relate to seasonal charts.
Reason for seasonal changes. Causes of floods.

Pattern
Dendritic or branching patterns made by water flows; rivers, deltas.

Water
Orders of streams. Water dissolves nutrients and pollution.
Moving water carries materials. Looking at river systems around the world.

Soil
Erosion, effect of mulching.

Plants
Recognising healthy and sick plants.

Animals
Shelter and homes and responses to flooding.

2. Basic skills and concepts appropriate to the grade level
Graphing local rainfall data.
Seasons.
Measuring and expressing
 duration of time.
Measuring liquid volumes in millilitres.
Subtraction to find comparative differences.
Library Research.
Reading historical and recent news
 items regarding flooding locally.
Writing a news item about
 the flood in the garden.
Map reading and using scale.

3. Values and behaviours
Listening to instructions. Remaining on task in the outdoors. Staying on task in the outdoors allows the task to be completed.
Valuing thorough and well planned designs (that, in this case, will reduce soil erosion).
Observation in the outdoors is an important part of the learning activities. People can learn from nature.

4. Area for special treatment
Grammar.
Adjectives; Identifying, listing and using
 suitable adjectives in written expression.
Mathematics; Scale drawing.

5. Processes to be emphasised
Observation, recording, reporting,
 researching (rainfall data),
 comparing, predicting, inquiry,
 identification and measurement.

Understandings
Past information can indicate a future problem. Water runs at 90 degrees (or close to) to contour.
Events have consequences to living and non-living things. Weather events have formed the world we know.
Understanding natural processes allows us to create good design for human settlement and food production.
Humans have always observed and reacted to natural forces. Keeping accurate records will help
 future generations to make better decisions. Consequences result from events and actions.

Vocabulary

Seasonal, unseasonal, dendritic, comparison, comparative, flood, deluge, inundated, momentum, force, sediment, sedimentation, storm, rain event, cyclone, dissolved, carried, humus.

Assessment Tools to be Used

1. Elementals

Drawing the map of the garden showing the observed water movement.
Observation record sheets/ journal entries.
Branching drawings.
Statement about the benefit of mulch, slowing water movement and working on contour.
Matching worksheet on plant health.
Report on an animal and its response to flooding (proactive and/ or reactive).

2. Basic skills

Bar and column graphs.
Matching activity showing links with rainfall figures and seasons.
Problems involving volume.
Report, presentation or talk from library research.
The class flood news items.
Newspaper article about the flooding of the school garden or bushland.

3. Values and behaviours

Worksheets completed correctly and on time.
Good suggestions to stop soil erosion by moving water.

4. Area for special treatment

The flood news report that contains appropriate adjectives.

List of Evidence to Gather

Newspaper article about the flood in the garden.
Comment in Garden Journal on the garden work, team work and participation levels.
Worksheets, journal entries.
Report or presentation.
Mathematical problems solved.
Branching pattern drawings.

Reporting and Evaluation

Reporting could be done through any of the linked Key Learning Areas. Particular reporting on any of the processes to be emphasised may support other observations on a report card or student record card.
A report to parents may be in the form of a presentation night for parents about the effect of a large rain event on the school and plans to mediate any future events. This may be part of a media study project.

Evaluation

For the evaluation the teacher may make comments here as to the value of the unit to students (overall and in particular learning areas).
Record here what worked or didn't work.
How it may be enhanced in the future and what activities may spin off from this unit.
State the appropriateness of the time allowed and any special outcomes.
Also record anything that would help a teacher at your school who wanted to either replicate the best aspects of the learning experiences, or who would want to follow on with another task in a subsequent year.

Title: Seeds; From Little Things Big Things Grow	Grade: Lower Primary	Duration: 4-8 weeks	Outdoor areas utilised: Vegetable garden, pots next to classroom, greenhouse

Overview

Finding seeds in fruit and vegetables. Identifying the part of a plant that is the seed.
Learning its role in the life cycle.
Planting found seeds into pots close to classroom or in the shade house.
Sprouting seeds to have with salad for lunch.
Listing seeds that are a valuable food source. Listing (graphing) the seeds we eat in our diet.
Comparing the size of a seed with the size of the full grown plant/ tree (Principle; use small and slow solutions.)
How seeds are spread (dispersed). Classifying seed according to size,
colour, shape, dispersal method or plant families.
Making a selection of seeds to plant. Understanding the needs of a seed.
Temperature, depth of soil, water requirements.
Understanding the needs of the emerging plant (nutrients, light, water, temperature, shelter).
Meeting the needs of a seed and growing it to a mature plant.

Scope of Curriculum Links

1. Elementals

Climate
Noting the best season for planting specific seeds. Most seeds germinate best in warm soil.

Pattern
The seed contains all the information for the adult plant. Seeds have a basic pattern with countless variations.

Water
Water is essential for the life of plants and for seeds to germinate.

Living Soil
Digging holes in preparation for planting seeds and seedlings. Basic importance of soil as providing support and nutrients.

Plants
Collecting seed for observation and identification.
Sprouting seeds. Growing plants from seed.
Not all plants have seeds for reproduction.

Trees
Identifying and collecting seed from trees.

Permaculture
Permaculture techniques provide clean and healthy food. Seed-saving is an ancient and essential activity.

2. Basic skills and concepts appropriate to the grade level

Science and Technology
The process of germination, life cycle, parts of a plant, efficient shapes and techniques for seed dispersal.
Linking seed dispersal design with inventions (helicopters, Velcro etc). Seed-saving techniques.

Mathematics
Counting and simple addition and subtraction which may extend to multiplication as repeated addition or to division as repeated subtraction. Cardinal and ordinal numbers (The 3rd seed is a lima bean etc). Odd and even numbers of seeds in fruit/ vegetables and picture graph the results.

Reading
Seed names and required growing conditions.
Related poems and literature. Following planting instructions. Reading 'The Little Red Hen'.

Writing
Lists of fruit, vegetable, tree seeds. Creative Writing - 'The Travels of the …Seed Before it Found its Home'.

Craft
Seed mosaic. Turning seed pods to useful objects such as containers, or musical instruments

Music
Making music with seed instruments. Learning songs about seeds and germination. Percussion instruments.

Other Cultures
Ancient and other cultures used seeds in different ways.

3. Values and behaviours

Small and slow solutions are best. (Read the 'Hare and the Tortoise Fable').
Learning from observing nature is lifelong education.
Seeds are invaluable as they cannot be invented or made by humans.
Seed-saving is an important job because human culture has relied on seed-saving (that will produce viable seed every generation) for thousands of years.

4. Area for special treatment	5. Processes to be emphasised
Counting and ordinal numbers. Solving problems with basic operations. Working in small groups. Manipulating small items and placing them in a planned position.	Observation, counting, classifying, measuring, manipulating, saving and storing, planting, germinating.

Understandings

We can save seed to grow new plants. Seeds contain information. This information is released on germination. Seeds have mechanisms for effective dispersal. These mechanisms can be observed and applied to meet design needs. Human culture has relied on agriculture that relies on seed-saving for ten thousand years. Viable seeds are vital for food production. Food production is essential for human health.

Vocabulary

Seed, seedling, germinate, germination, sprouting, plant, information, outside, inside, small, large (the comparative adjectives - small, smaller, smallest). Descriptive words such as hard, soft, round, oval, brown, black, waxy, coated, contains, sow, reap, grow.

Assessment Tools to be Used

1. Elementals	2. Basic skills

Work sheets;
  matching the seed to the plant, selecting the best comparative adjective.
Photographic record;
  children and their seed collection and their own classification system.
Teacher checklists;
  understands that seeds are living things, that they contain all the information of the adult plant, works well in small groups to collect, germinate, plant seeds.
Poster or drawing: The Seed of the Week.
Plant and nurture the growing plant to full growth or acceptable level of successful maturity.
	Matching seed picture with a dispersal method drawing.
	Counting and performing simple mathematical operations with seeds to the appropriate level. Collecting and categorising seeds for the class seed bank.
	Graphing favourite fruits as a picture graph or bar graph.
	Creating lists (plant names, materials needed for sprouting or germinating). Class book or individual stories (dictated or written) about the adventures of a seed.
	Reading simple names and planting recommendations. (To appropriate level)
	Seed picture (demonstrating manipulative skill).
	Musical instrument made with seeds.

3. Values and behaviours	4. Area for special treatment
Seeds are a valuable resource. Organised storage makes finding things later easier. (Seed bank). A job well done ensures a good result. Co-operative group work. Organisation. Good work ethic.	Mathematics is linked to real authentic situations and the children use it spontaneously as a tool to solve real life problems. Children showing more respect for living things and meeting the needs of the plants/ seeds without instruction. Improved manipulative skills with small items.

List of Evidence to Gather

Work sheets, solutions to mathematical questions or problems, a labelled seed collection, lists of seeds, a planted area of garden or planter box, a piece of art or craft that uses seed pods as a container or medium. Teacher worksheets and photos.

Reporting and Evaluation

Reporting on the work in this unit may be included in statements about all Key Learning Areas. Specific reporting may be entered under a special topic 'School Garden and Sustainability'. Comments about understandings, skills and behaviours will give parents and subsequent teachers an understanding of strengths as well as areas that need further practice. Video and other presentations to parents at special events will also give the opportunity to showcase the garden and basic skills' acquisition.

Evaluation

Comments about the resources, times required for the germination activities, effectiveness of worksheets and assessment methods will provide valuable information when doing this unit again or for other teachers that will incorporate it into their program in the future.

Title: Patterns in Nature (The Fibonacci Numbers)	Grade: Upper Primary	Duration: 2 weeks	Outdoor areas utilised: Flower garden Vegetable Garden

Overview

Children will explore the outdoors to find and 'classify' found patterns (Set theory). It is anticipated that two of the patterns will be spirals and branching patterns. These both reflect the Fibonacci series.
Collecting pictures and found objects that have the spiral or branching pattern.
Placing in categories, making sets and overlapping sets (Venn Diagrams).
Exploring the mathematics behind the natural spiral pattern and finding the Fibonacci series (1, 2, 3, 5, 8, 13.....).
Drawing a spiral through squares of ascending Fibonacci numbers.
Searching for the Fibonacci numbers in flowers, in the petal numbers.
Using the Fibonacci series and/ or numbers in artistic works. (Observational drawings or pattern making.)
Using various media to show pattern use and recording of patterns in nature such as charcoal and lino cuts or positive and negative cuts from coloured paper. (Pattern as predictable repetitions.)
Making collections of items and events that exhibit the Fibonacci series.
Animals that use spirals (The Molluscs).
Spirals in plants (unfurled fern fronds).

Scope of Curriculum Links

1. Elementals
Finding fractals.
Patterns in winds (The Eckman Spiral).
Pattern in water (The Von Karmen Trail).
Locating and identifying patterns in moving air or water that affect the schoolyard.
Finding the windy and sheltered spots.
Designing a windbreak or finding Fibonacci numbers in petals or seeds (sunflowers).
Identifying that same pattern in the bioregion, describing it, drawing or photographing it, commenting on its usefulness or how its effects may be enhanced or modified.
Design a living fence that will shelter a playground area.

2. Basic skills and concepts appropriate to the grade level
Mathematics
Number series and patterns. Sets and intersecting sets.
Researching the pattern form and function (library and internet). Ratio.
Calculating the next number in the Fibonacci series. (Addition exercises.)
Creating a number pattern and working out five repetitions.
Science
Phylum of Molluscs and the spiral form.
Art
Golden ratio in famous art works.
Creating repetitive patterns.
Line drawings (or rubbings)of leaf and branch patterns.

3. Values and behaviours
Mathematics is useful to make sense of the world.
There are links between all living and non living things and these can be expressed in mathematical formula.
We can apply lessons from nature that can benefit our lives. We can learn by observing. Nature teaches valuable lessons.

4. Area for special treatment
Making mathematics interesting and working with numbers other than in basic operations and problem solving.
Magic squares. Numbers in nature, the golden ratio as it applies to architecture and painting.
Other discoveries of Leonardo daVinci.
The Mandelbrot Set.

5. Processes to be emphasised
Observation, counting, predicting, classifying, describing, researching, reporting.

Understandings
Patterns are predictable repetitions. They appear in nature in many forms and varieties.
Natural patterns perform functions. Humans can copy the appropriate pattern to perform a desired function.
Humans make sense of the world through mathematics.
Working with nature requires less energy and resources than working against nature.

Vocabulary

Words that describe pattern and shape such as dendritic, fractal, nets, spiral, repeat, replicable, Phylum, molluscs, repetitive, nautilus shell, branching, dendrologist, rivers, tributaries, espalier.

Assessment Tools to be Used

1. Elementals

Student diary and journal with record of observations.
Lists of plants with Fibonacci numbers as petal numbers.
Lists of fruits and vegetables that follow the Fibonacci series pattern.
Description (report or poster) of a pattern in the school or that affects the schoolyard.
Windbreak design.
Pattern in the region; photographs and report, video report.

2. Basic skills

Teacher checklist indicating children's ability to classify items, form sets.
Photos of categories.
Quiz or matching activity that show the child can predict the next number in a series.
Meaningful practice for the operation of addition (3+5=8, 5+8=13, 8+13= 21 etc).
Drawings of sets and intersecting sets.
Artworks that show repetitions as pattern.
Using a pattern to make a craft object (repeatable).
Report/ poster on a selected mollusc.
Written descriptions of plant or animal patterns.
Measuring the golden ratio. Estimating the golden ratio.
Listing famous artworks and buildings that use the golden ratio.

3. Values and behaviours

Teacher observation of attitude and behavioural changes in mathematics' lessons.
Teacher checklist of observational skills.

4. Area for special treatment
Mathematics

Making links to nature in lessons in mathematics' and referring to maths in garden and art lessons.
Increased accuracy and speed in addition.

List of Evidence to Gather

Diary, journal, photographs.
Teacher checklists – interest in mathematics, observational skills.
Reports, posters, lists.
Design of a windbreak.
Drawings, Quiz, Matching activities.
Written expression and research to appropriate level.
Accuracy and speed test in addition.

Reporting and Evaluation

Reporting in this unit may cross many subject area boundaries. These may be Art, Craft, Mathematics, Science (Biology, Geography or Botany), Reading, Writing (in several genres), observational skills, reporting/ media skills, research skills and so on.
So checklists and products would be an effective form of reporting along with student self-assessment.
Evaluation
This is where you discuss what worked and what didn't, how you could use it in future, how to build on the work in this unit and any specific tasks that need further work.
It is a valuable section for improving the unit for next time and for seeing the links to other subject areas.

Suggested Unit Titles

1. Seasonal Change
   (To Autumn, Winter, Spring, Summer)
2. Patterns in Nature (The Dendritic Pattern)
3. After the Storm
4. Plants that are Good to Eat
   (Yummy Tucker)
5. Craft From the Garden (Musical, instruments, corn dollies, scarecrows)
6. Recycling Our Waste
7. Building a Herb Spiral
8. Worms
9. The Energy We Use
10. Our Water Wise Garden
11. Bushland Friends
12. Fabulous Fruits
13. Critters
14. Helpers in the Garden (bees, butterflies, birds, lizards)
15. Chooks
16. Something Fishy or Little Ponds
17. Soils Ain't Soils
18. Gardens in the Desert
19. Growing in Cold Climates
20. Adapting to Climate
21. Local Resources

Teachers will be able to come up with hundreds more depending on resources and the needs of the children.

Part V

Odds and sods

Brainstorms

Edward De Bono's *'Six Thinking Hats'*, 1985, is a technique useful in the first stages of discussions about a new project. It is a technique for running a brainstorming session – a framework upon which to build the discussion.

It involves six coloured hats (figuratively speaking) each with a distinct function eg the White Hat is concerned with the objective, the facts and figures. The group is asked to brainstorm the neutral information that applies to the topic. They then move on to Red Hat thinking to give their emotional responses to the concept. These cover things that might make them angry or annoyed. The Black Hat covers the negatives – why it can't be done. The Yellow Hat is sunny and positive and this includes all the hopes people have for the project. The Green Hat is creative and here the new ideas for growth and change are recorded. The Blue Hat represents the sky, the overarching view, and here discussion is about summaries, conclusions and where-to-next ideas.

The following is a copy of a brainstorming session for a school garden project for a primary school. It may be useful if you are using the technique for the first time. The sequence of the 'hats' is optional. Some prefer to begin with the Red Hat. The information in it is only a guide to the process and we encourage you to voice your own thoughts.

White Hat for facts and figures.
The position is neutral and objective
- obesity in children is rising
- nutritional choice is poor
- understanding of food issues limited
- rise in mental disorders eg ADHD
- children's play is constantly supervised
- children learn new technologies quickly
- we are losing skills in old technologies
- childhood is played out indoors
- bullying is a problem
- school grounds cater mostly for sport
- A lot of land is tied up in school grounds
- entertainment is mostly screen-based
- children like to be outdoors at school
- they prefer practical alternatives to talking
- we are all facing serious environmental issues
- children need fresh air
- children are learning indoors

Red Hat for the emotions. What are your reactions, hunches and impressions? What makes you angry or annoyed?
- the school day is already overloaded
- I am sick of change. This is just another
- it will be too expensive to set up
- schools are putting litigation issues ahead of the good of the child
- there will be strong resistance to change
- teachers are indifferent about gardens
- this could be good for the children who are disruptive in the classroom
- do I have to do it?
- school grounds are underdeveloped
- school grounds are barren
- schoolyards are compacted and sterile
- teachers will not get involved
- there are enough interruptions to the school day as it is
- there is nowhere for my child to play at lunch time

171

Black Hat for gloomy and negative responses

- workplace health and safety issues will be a barrier to success
- what happens when the teacher leaves the school
- who will look after it in the holidays
- the garden will attract the wrong people into the schoolyard
- gardening would be a distraction to the work at hand
- it is uncomfortable outside
- there are many children with allergies
- I can't see any good reason to garden at school

Yellow Hat for positive thoughts about school gardens

- children need to be part of the solution to the problems we face
- they need to know about good food for their well being
- they can learn to grow and prepare their own food
- the learning can be curriculum based
- the garden is a place for children to learn
- the garden is a place of enjoyment
- some children will learn best in the garden
- learning can be 'hands-on'
- children can be experimental
- learning is real-life, not abstract
- there is help in the community
- we should see what other schools are doing

Green Hat for new ideas. This is where people can be creative and 'fly high' with ideas

- each class could have a garden project
- composting at school is easy
- there is money available
- we could apply for funds
- I would like to see many different types of gardens
- we could build an outdoor classroom
- we could introduce animals

- we could improve the environmental quality of the schoolyard
- we could 'soften' the school landscape
- we could remove some of the asphalt

Blue Hat is for summarising the discussion and deciding how to go forward

- the general feel of this meeting is for positive action
- we should form a committee to take the process forward
- we will need to talk to all stakeholders including the children

The Six Thinking Hats approach is a proven strategy to streamline thinking. It has been applied successfully in diverse situations – corporate, administration, government and teaching – any situation that involves group decision-making. The technique is taught to children in some schools to improve their thinking skills.

The food garden at school

Tips for an easy start

- start small
- brainstorm design ideas and site choice with the children
- place it close to the classroom or shelter shed for frequent access
- site close to a water source
- do simple soil tests
- make no-dig beds using sheet-mulching techniques
- plant vegetables, herbs and flowers
- choose perennials and biennials as well as annuals
- choose self-seeding plants for permanence
- help children do the work

Make a no-dig garden (sheet-mulching)

Gather as much free stuff as you can

- newspaper
- sawdust
- compost
- old manures
- old bricks for edging and paths
- timber for edging
- strawberry runners
- seedlings

Planting

- choose plants suited to your region
- plant at the right time
- be aware of growth habits

- start with punnets of seedlings or seeds germinated in the classroom
- punnets of four or six plants are easy for children to handle
- gloves are not needed, nailbrushes are
- make it a cheerful event, photograph it, begin a log
- give all the children a job even it is only to watch and report

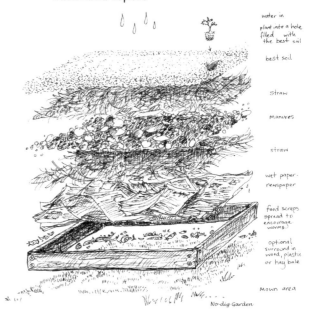

water in
plant into a hole filled with the best soil
best soil
Straw
manures
straw
wet paper-newspaper
food scraps spread to encourage worms
optional surround in wood, plastic or hay bale
Mown area
No-dig Garden

Children like to grow and eat

- cherry tomatoes
- peas and beans
- strawberries
- parsley
- lettuce
- blueberries

Stop to celebrate

- gather round to officially launch the new garden
- name it and wish it well on its way to a good yield
- promise to care for it and to not pick anything until it is ready
- tell other children the rules of the garden
- take lots of photos and notes

Expansion

When the first bed is working and the children are impatiently waiting for their first crop, this may be a good time to extend the garden.

Some ideas

- build another no-dig bed
- make a path between the two
- grow a vine crop such as pumpkins, cucumber, rock melon
- extend the range of annuals – corn, beetroot, chinese cabbage, roma tomatoes

Techniques

- rotate the crops around the garden, it is a good idea not to plant the same vegetable in the same spot in the next season
- water the garden with saved water if possible
- reduce weeds by covering the soil with mulch
- consider companion planting

    asparagus + beans + basil + tomatoes

    radish + carrot

    corn + beans

    cabbages + tomatoes

Additions that children love

- paths and trails
- fruit trees and vines
- herb and flower gardens
- ponds and chickens
- worm beds and compost heaps
- water tanks and potting areas
- fences and tipi trellises
- art and craft work in the garden
- scarecrows
- composting bins or bays
- potato farms
- places to play in the dirt and big shady trees
- rocks and sawdust
- hidey holes and cubbies
- nursery
- story telling tree
- big garden seat for the teacher…

For more ideas see graphic of 'features for your school garden' on page 97

How to make it their garden

- be excited for the children
- choose the plants that they like to eat
- plants that grow fast are good: lettuce, radish, sunflowers
- tools should be real and not play things
- kid size gloves for composting, bare hands for planting
- paths and edges are fun and trust them to design these
- give them all an important job
- celebrate and make it feel important

Garden Rules

Children need guidance to act appropriately in the garden. Without some understanding of the needs of the plants, they are capable of undoing a lot of good work. The following are rules that can be placed in the classroom and on signs in the garden. Signs with humour appeal to everyone eg Trespassers will be Composted

- Do not walk over my bed, thank you
- I am not ready to be picked or Don't Pick Me I am not ready to be eaten
- Do not disturb. Plants are sleeping in their beds
- Children at Work
- Do not play with your food
- If flowers were friends, I'd pick you
- Bean there Dug that
- Give peas a chance
- Climb like a monkey Don't fall like a brick

This is just a sample of signs that you can add to the garden to guide the children's behaviour. The children need to know how to behave in the garden and the more humour that you can put into the signage, the better.

Conclusion

A garden in every school may well be a mandate for principals in the future. Enthusiasm is building for this outdoor classroom as permaculture/food/kitchen/edible gardens, imbedded in learning programs, are springing up all over the country and teachers are reporting favourable outcomes from the activities.

There is overwhelming evidence from those who are pioneering this educational landscape that gardens provide a wide range of effective learning experiences that support many aspects of the curriculum including environmental education for sustainability. School gardens are proving to be an effective setting for ecological understanding, awareness of food and health issues, skills and values building and learning in the core subjects of the curiculum. The technique is experiential learning and teachers are reclaiming the wisdom that children learn by 'doing'.

The positive potential of the school garden to support children's learning is being unlocked as teachers explore the teaching and learning opportunities of the site.

Just as Jack climbed the beanstalk to another world, children can follow the growth of their garden to a place of rich rewards. By making a vegetable patch, they will see the way nature works. It may well help them to understand themselves; who they are, where they are going and what they can do. They can learn and practise acts of self-reliance and resourcefulness and make a contribution to a quality of life for themselves and others.

There are rich rewards for the teacher who climbs the beanstalk with the kids. A school garden is filled with the lessons of life and living and there are riches within for the teacher who chooses to step outside. The outdoor classroom is on your doorstep.

Happy gardening

References

Alexander, S, Kitchen Garden Cooking for Kids, Penguin, Australia 2006

Cushing, H, Beyond Organics, Gardening for the Future, ABC Books, Sydney, 2005

Cox, M, Imagine.... School Grounds as 'Learnscapes', My Coot-tha Botanic Gardens, 1991

Deans, E, Gardening Book: Growing Without Digging, Harper and Son, Sydney. 1977

Deans, E, Leaves of Light, Harper Collins, Australia, 1991

Dewey, J, Democracy and Education, Macmillan, London, 1916

Education for a Sustainable Future, Commonwealth of Australia, 2005

De Bono, E, Six Thinking Hats, Penguin, London. 1985

Fanton, J, and Immig, J, Seed to Seed: Food Gardens in Schools, The Seed Savers Network, Byron Bay, 2007

French, J, Companion Planting, Aird Books, Melbourne, 1991

French, J, Soil Food, Avid Book, Melbourne, 1995

Gardener, H, Multiple Intelligences: The Theory in Practice, USA, 1993

Glasser, W, Choice Theory: A New Pedagogy of Personal Freedom, Harper Collins. 1998

Heinberg, R, The Party's Over, New Society Publishers, Canada, 2003

Holmgren, D, Permaculture Principles and Pathways Beyond Sustainability, Permanent Publications, UK, 2002

Lancaster, B, Rainwater Harvesting for Drylands, Rainsource Press. Arizona, 2006

Lovelock, J, The Revenge of Gaia. Allen Lane, UK, 2006

Mars, R, Getting Started in Permaculture, Permanent Publications, UK, 1988

Mars, R, The Basics of Permaculture Design, Permanent Publications, UK, 2003

Mollison, B, Holmgren, D, Permaculture One, Transworld Publishers. Australia, 1978

Mollison, B Permaculture Two, Tagari, Australia, 1979

Mollison, B, Permaculture: A Designers' Manual, Tagari, Tyalgum, Australia, 1998

Mollison, B, Introduction to Permaculture, Tagari, Tyalgum 1991

Morrow, R, Earth User's Guide to Permaculture, Permanent Publications, UK, 2006

Nuttall, C, A Children's Food Forest: An Outdoor Classroom, Fefl Books, Australia, 1996

Tate, C, The Influence of Trees in the Classroom on Learning, SFA Arboretum, Texas, USA

The Unschooled Mind: How Children Think and Schools Should Teach. Basic Books, 1993

Van Matre, S, Earth Education A New Beginning, The Institute of Earth Education, West Virginia, USA, 1990

White, M, The Nature of Hidden Worlds, Reed, Chatswood,1990

Whitehead, G (ed), Planting the Nation, Australian Garden History Society, Victoria, 2001

Wise, T, Gardens for Children, Kangaroo Press, Kenthurst, 1986

Woodward, P, Vardy, P, Community Gardens, Hyland House, Victoria, 2005